Discrimination, Harassment, and the Failure of Diversity Training

Discrimination, Harassment, and the Failure of Diversity Training

What to Do Now

Hellen Hemphill
and Ray Haines

QUORUM BOOKS
Westport, Connecticut • London

Library of Congress Cataloging-in-Publication Data

Hemphill, Hellen, 1933–
    Discrimination, harassment, and the failure of diversity training :
what to do now / by Hellen Hemphill and Ray Haines.
        p.   cm.
    Includes bibliographical references and index.
    ISBN 1–56720–109–1 (alk. paper)
    1. Diversity in the workplace.   2. Discrimination.   3. Sexual
harassment.   I. Haines, Ray, 1933–   .   II. Title.
HF5549.5.M5H458   1997
658.3'145—DC21   97–1702

British Library Cataloguing in Publication Data is available.

Library of Congress Catalog Card Number: 97–1702
ISBN: 1–56720–109–1

First published in 1997

Quorum Books, 88 Post Road West, Westport, CT 06881
An imprint of Greenwood Publishing Group, Inc.

Printed in the United States of America

The paper used in this book complies with the
Permanent Paper Standard issued by the National
Information Standards Organization (Z39.48–1984).

10 9 8 7 6 5 4 3 2

We offer our thanks and dedicate this book to our loving spouses:

Marilyn Haines and Dale Hemphill,

who encouraged and supported us, adding their wisdom and unique suggestions as we struggled to clarify the solution to the workplace dilemma.

It must be remembered that there is nothing more difficult to plan, or doubtful of success, nor more dangerous to manage than the creation of a new system.

For the initiator has the enmity of all who would profit by the preservation of the old institution and merely lukewarm defenders in those who would gain by the new ones.

—Machiavelli, *The Prince,* 1513

Contents

viii   Contents

Preface

We found it difficult to begin writing this book because for the last decade we both had been deeply entrenched in the diversity training movement and because of the many dedicated individuals we have met inside and outside of organizations who earnestly supported the diversity training premise. They sincerely believed that teaching workers to understand, appreciate, and value their unique differences would foster an environment in which each individual would be honored and respected, and that through this diversity training process discrimination and harassment would be diminished and eventually eliminated.

Literally, days were spent considering the personal and professional consequences of challenging the current premise. We finally decided that someone had to say it: *Diversity training has failed to eliminate discrimination and harassment in the workplace.* In fact, it has created even more divisiveness and disruption than existed before. A major course correction is needed.

Diversity training programs failed because of their focus on awareness, understanding and appreciating differences, rather than on teaching the basic skills needed to relate effectively to one another in the workplace. It is useful to recognize and acknowledge our unique differences, but it is far more essential to address effective and appropriate workplace behaviors. This conflict of solutions in the elimination of discrimination and harassment behaviors became a workplace dilemma.

Our solution to this dilemma acknowledges that organizations cannot effectively force changes in values or attitudes, but they can mandate appropriate workplace behaviors. We recommend that all organizations adopt and enforce a zero tolerance policy for discrimination and harassment practices, provide and publish a set of acceptable and unacceptable workplace behavior standards, and offer a training program in workplace relationship skills for all employees.

The authors welcome comments and discussion regarding the solution to the elimination of discrimination and harassment that is spelled out in this book. Please make contact through their e-mail address or visit our web site:

Hellen Hemphill, P.D., and Ray Haines

E-mail: xray@nwlink.com
or
Web Site: http://www.transition-s.com

Acknowledgments

A special thanks to Susan Mersereau, vice president of Weyerhaeuser Company, Federal Way, Washington, and Gerald McGuire, president of McGuire & Associates, White Rock, British Columbia, for their valuable suggestions in forming the final outline of our solution for eliminating of discrimination and harassment in the workplace. We also extend our deepest appreciation to the following who have read our initial draft and have provided insightful feedback: Jackie Allen, Virginia Anderson, Charles Collins, Cynthia Flash, Donna Fothe, Shirley Grulke, Yoshio Hara, Alice Harris, Dennis Jaffe, Rich Long, Bob Ogdon, Dorothy Paul, Thelma Reynaga, Don Saunders, Deborah Terry-Hays, and Robert Terry. Ongoing conversations with numerous other executives who participated in a 1992 national diversity summit implemented by Hellen Hemphill increased her awareness of the limitations of diversity training programs and the rampant discrimination and harassment practices continuing inside U.S. organizations.

Thanks to the members of the Iowa City Human Rights Commission and those individuals who brought their discrimination and harassment cases for review and action by the Commission. They provided Ray Haines with the impetus to lead the development of the REACH for Excellence Workplace Diversity Program. Contributors and participants of this program, too numerous to name, deserve our thanks for their influence on Ray's understanding of diversity training's failure to eliminate discrimination and harassment practices in the workplace. Ray also expresses a special debt of gratitude for the opportunity to share with and gain feedback from the players and their spouses of his life long poker group.

We acknowledge the fine work of Greenwood Publishing Company's editorial staff: Norine Mudrick, our production editor, for the excellent support and helpful recommendations; former vice president James R. Ice for believing in us; vice president Lynn Taylor for taking on the subsequent leadership role; and

Doug Goldenberg-Hart, the product manager of marketing, for developing our national marketing thrust.

Thanks to Rich Long for an excellent final edit; to our dedicated and creative book editor Claudia McCormick, who made it possible for us to meet our initial publishing deadline with a book that we are proud to publish; to Sharon Bolton for her expertise in editing and shaping the book; and to Mary Dispenza for her early contribution to the development of the book.

Special appreciation is given to all members of our families for their continual encouragement, dedication, love, and support.

1

The Workplace Dilemma

INTRODUCTION

In November 1996 two major stories that hit the news speak to the timeliness and importance of this book. Texaco paid a record settlement of $176.1 million in a racial discrimination suit, and the U.S. Army was confronted with potential sexual harassment claims from over 5,000 women. Both of these organizations had implemented diversity training, and that training failed.

In spite of diversity training's well-intended efforts to eliminate discrimination and harassment in the workplace, they continue. In the past decade alone, American businesses have spent billions of dollars on diversity training in an effort to eliminate extensive discrimination and harassment practices in the workplace. Hundreds of millions of dollars more have been spent on legal fees.

In 1994, we began questioning top business executives in sixty-five major companies about their diversity training experiences. Disenchantment with diversity training programs was rampant. Typical of those discussions were the following comments:

Every white man in my workforce went ballistic over the diversity training program I brought in last month. Prior to the training, the trainer described her content to me, and when she went into that session, she did something very different! I'm not going to let that happen again.

We hired what we thought was the best diversity trainer in the country. She led this program where everyone was asked to share their stereotypes about gays, women, blacks, and others. People were extremely upset! Many of them went away traumatized, not talking to each other for months. I even got calls at home. Some of those stereotypes were used in a discrimination lawsuit against the company. It cost our company millions of dollars.

I'm not wasting my people's time trying to change the way they "feel" about people who are different from them. If there is a problem, just tell us what you want us to do. Don't waste our time with this diversity stuff.

The problem was readily apparent, but the solution had not yet surfaced—there was more to learn.

Stephen M. Paskoff describes diversity programs as "a waste of valuable time . . . a huge perception gap, one that persists despite all the diversity programs aimed at helping workers empathize with those who are 'different'." He continues: "The pervasiveness of that stubborn perception gap suggests that the achievements of most corporate diversity training programs have been superficial at best. And how could it be otherwise when these programs attempt to bridge enormous sociological divides that are beyond the ability of any business organization to repair?" [1]

The evidence is overwhelming that diversity training programs have failed to significantly reduce discrimination and harassment in the workplace. In many cases, diversity training caused further divisiveness and negative labeling. As a result of this failure, many organizational leaders and diversity professionals are caught up in conflicting solutions for reducing and eliminating the deeply embedded discrimination and harassment behaviors in their workplace environments.

To compete in this decade's changing national and global business markets, organizational leaders must be able to count on the loyalty and top performance of all their employees. They can do this only if the workplace is freed from the profound, limiting, and debilitating effects of discrimination and harassment on their workers. Discrimination falls into four basic areas:

- *Isolated discrimination*: Intentionally harmful actions undertaken by a dominant group member against members of a subordinate group, without that action being socially embedded in the larger organization or community context;
- *Small group discrimination*: Intentionally harmful actions undertaken by a few dominant group members acting in concert against members of subordinate groups, without the sanction of the larger organization;
- *Direct institutional discrimination*: Organizationally prescribed actions that, by intention, have a negative impact upon members of subordinate groups which are routine actions carried out by large numbers of employees guided by organizational norms and culture; and
- *Indirect institutional discrimination*: Practices that have a negative impact upon members of a subordinate group—even though the prescribed norms and regulations guiding these actions were established with no intent to harm subordinate group members. [2]

All four kinds of discrimination cost companies a high price, as well as good employee and customer relations. It cost Denny's restaurants $1 billion in wages and revenues for discrimination against blacks. Miller Brewing Company reached a $1.7 million settlement with its black employees. Black females and Hispanic employees won a huge discrimination suit from the Lucky stores. Over the past twenty-five years, there has been a 2,100 percent increase in discrimination suits heard in federal courts. [3] According to U.S. Merit Systems Protection Board data published in 1995, sexual harassment cost the U.S. government, the nation's largest employer, an estimated $327 million dollars during the two-year period, April 1992 to April 1994. This amount includes the cost of sick leave, job turnover, and productivity losses. Cost to private industry is similarly high. Enlightened business leaders today look for an effective solution to these expensive problems. [4]

This dilemma was intensified by the pressure to address human rights malpractice that had been placed on organizations from society and governmental regulations and mandates, such as affirmative action, equal employment opportunity, or the Americans with Disabilities Act (ADA). The destructive impact of demeaning human rights practices on worker retention, effectiveness, and productivity was brought to national attention by the media. As a consequence, most government agencies and over 60 percent of Fortune 500 companies currently engage in some sort of diversity training, ranging from one-time lectures and videos to three-day "experiential" training workshops.

Diversity training hoped to find a solution to these challenging human rights problems. Not only did it fail, but it left havoc and wreckage in its wake. From that despair, hopelessness, and confusion emerged the "workplace dilemma." Employees continually deal with, avoid, deny, dance around, or struggle with the detrimental effects of discrimination and harassment. This difficult problem has been a part of organizations since the beginning of modern business. It has not gone away; it has only been made worse.

This is an issue that provokes strong emotions in most people, running the gamut from guilt to burning rage Our country still separates people of color, gender, and sexual orientation and accords them second-class citizenship. Even the progress that has been made against discrimination is seldom acknowledged. The privileged status of the white male causes outrage; conversely, white males are outraged that their status has diminished. Those sensitive to the issues at hand experience shame and guilt that so little has changed since the days of the Emancipation Proclamation. The passion inherent in these matters makes it difficult to continue "business as usual." Organizations that have tried to address these issues have witnessed painful and traumatic confrontations among their managers and their workforce. We have reopened old wounds and created new ones. These sores are left to fester without solutions to heal them.

THE DEMISE OF THE DIVERSITY TRAINING SOLUTION

Because of economic, social, and legal pressures, many organizations gladly opened their doors to diversity training. The initial purpose of diversity training was to help women and minorities, some placed in organizations as a result of affirmative action, adjust to the workplace culture—and to help the work-place culture adjust to them. Diversity training's primary intent was to raise human consciousness and to reduce and eventually eliminate discrimination and harassment practices toward women and minorities. Trainers expected to fulfill this purpose by teaching the value of human differences. It was thought, and sincerely so, that if employees understood one another's differences, then discrimination and harassment would be reduced. With new-found understanding, sympathetic employees would work together more effectively and productively.

In 1995 alone, there were as many as 5,000 self-proclaimed experts selling their wares as diversity trainers and consultants. Most of them were women and ethnic minority trainers and consultants who took up the diversity banner in the hopes of making a positive impact. Human resource managers we interviewed at that time said they received up to thirty brochures a week from diversity specialists hawking their particular brand of cultural awareness. It was a new field and consequently had no regulation or certification process. Anyone could buy or rent an agenda—including videotapes, manuals, and games. Long-term contracts with large organizations brought consultants in at up to a half a million dollars a year. The situation has yet to change. [5]

In response to diversity training's initial purpose, diversity professionals placed their emphasis on teaching a broad approach to differences: history, cultures, ethnicity, gender, and race. The training content was later expanded to include all differences such as age, disabilities, politics, religion, sexual orientation, and values. Sensitive issues of bias, scapegoating, prejudice, discrimination, harassment, oppression, and stereotyping became a part of the trainer's agenda. Diversity programs recommended applying individualized communication strategies based on every employee's group identity. Different cultures had different rules to cover a vast number of areas. In spite of its positive intent, it was unrealistic to think that with three to five hours of diversity training, complex sociological and cultural principles could be clearly understood, much less applied to all interpersonal relationships.

However unrealistic those hopes might have been, organizations continued to hire diversity consultants and trainers in the name of buying social peace. What was often purchased instead was more social conflict. This social conflict was created from the attempt to deal publicly with sensitive personal and social human rights issues better dealt with elsewhere. [6] Conflict intensified when the dominant group (the white males) was openly confronted by the minority group in these forums. Because a large number of diversity trainers were women and members of minority groups, many personal agendas, minority platforms, and social conflicts were frequently major portions of the program. This sowed the seeds of a hostile national backlash from white males.

White males report that they are tired of being made to feel guilty in every discussion of diversity. They are tired of being cast as the oppressors. Glen Collins, writing in *Self* magazine, says, "Young and old men are reacting against the Demonic White European Male syndrome, the perceived opinion that white males are responsible for every ill." [7]

Far from bringing estranged groups closer together, diversity exercises outraged many workers. In addition, members of the groups that already felt oppressed left the diversity programs feeling even more vulnerable and victimized. The wedge between employees widened and made working relationships worse than ever.

Reverse discrimination cries were heard all across America. A 1996 study by Princeton Survey Associates found that by a two-to-one margin—39 percent to 18 percent—more voters believe that reverse discrimination against whites is a bigger problem than racism. But 78 percent of employed white voters do not think they would have a better shot at promotion if they were of a different color. [8]

David Hartman, a male federal employee, filed a federal lawsuit under Title VII of the Civil Rights Act against the providers of his organization's three-day diversity training program, the Hart Performance Group. The complaint alleged civil rights violations that include sexual harassment, debasing of religion by a government-sponsored workshop, and continued retaliation and loss of promotion opportunity with the agency as a result of his filing a complaint. The announcement of this suit created a reverse-harassment media blitz in December of 1994. [9] Another well-publicized filing was the reverse-sex-discrimination suit of eight male employees against Jenny Craig Company. [10]

Our conclusion that diversity training programs have failed has been drawn from discussions with over 500 organizational executives, managers, and directors; conversations with more than 100 inside and outside diversity consultants and trainers; an in-depth search of workforce literature; and examination of media coverage on diversity issues over a five-year span. The evidence is overwhelming and our conclusion inevitable. Here is what our resources revealed regarding diversity training programs:

- Participants found many training programs divisive, disturbing, and counterproductive;
- Diversity trainers were often inexperienced and ineffective;
- Minority groups' expectations were raised, and then disappointed;
- White males were stereotyped and blamed;
- There was reverse discrimination and reverse stereotyping;
- A nationwide backlash occurred against diversity training programs;
- Sensitive and personal issues were brought out in hostile public settings;
- Workers experienced unnecessary anxiety and emotional upheaval;
- Increased distrust was engendered;
- Many workers were resistant to attending further diversity training programs; and

• Little or no transfer of learning took place from teaching about differences to changing discriminatory and harassing behaviors.

A prominent, national diversity consultant, expert, and author stated that more than 40 percent of the employees in most organizations who were forced to attend remained closed to the potential learning experience and refused to actually take part in diversity training classes or workshops. Many organizational respondents to our 1995 study questioned the value of presenting diversity awareness training at all. An executive of the AT&T School of Management Studies stated during a 1992 national diversity summit that AT&T chose to stop offering "diversity awareness" classes because women and minorities were the only ones attending. A "preaching to the choir" mentality emerged and training often became a divisive force as differences were once again accentuated. [11] Frederick R. Lynch, in his 1997 book, *The Diversity Machine: The Drive to Change the "White Male Workplace,"* comments that, ". . . diversity management still appears to be, and largely is, a human resource ghetto for victim-mongering blacks and women, humored and patronized by savvy CEOs who were obviously using diversity training as a talisman against discrimination lawsuits." [12] The way this diversity training drama played out set the stage for the solution to the workplace dilemma.

THE WORKPLACE CULTURE

With diversity training's failure, professionals are faced with the dilemma of finding a more effective solution to freeing the workplace of discrimination and harassment practices. However, the following factors inherent in the workplace preclude working toward an effective solution.

Denial of Discrimination and Harassment Problems

Many organizations deny the existence of discrimination and harassment in their workplaces. A vice president of one of the largest companies in the nation stated that he couldn't see what this diversity fuss was all about. He did not believe that his company had a significant problem with discrimination and harassment behaviors. In contrast, many of the company's women and minority employees reported to us a very different picture of this workplace environment. They described a male-dominated company with no women or minorities in senior management. A minority female stated that this lack of sensitivity to discrimination and harassment practices is typical at the top since little attention was paid to women and minority issues in this workplace. One of the company's top human resource representatives declared the organization to be one of the most archaic in the nation regarding human rights issues. [13]

In our interviews, women and minority employees from all types of organizations described discrimination and harassment practices as "alive and well" in their workplaces. Many of the white males we spoke to also described instances of discrimination (reverse discrimination) as a result of affirmative action programs.

Employee Loyalties, Values, and Belief Systems

America's workplace is a mosaic of races, religious groups, political parties, sexual orientations, and ethnic and gender groups. Loyalties to special interest groups cause people to polarize or band together. The many examples of this behavior in the news today include Republican, Democratic, and independent political parties; the Anita Hill and Clarence Thomas confrontation; the Rodney King case; U.S. Navy's Tailhook Harassment case; Margarethe Cammermeyer's Army discharge and reinstatement; the O.J. Simpson trial; Admiral Everett Greene's harassment trial and acquittal; and the beating of illegal immigrants by the San Diego police force. These social ills caused by identifying with specific interest groups are carried over to and reflected in the workplace.

The Mores of the Workplace Culture

Culture is the learned process behavior of group experience and contains unwritten rules of social conduct. Mores, which are these unwritten rules of behavior, are established by the dominant group. A few examples of how hidden bias or prejudice translates into behaviors that define workplace behaviors might be: (1) Don't bring your personal problems to work; (2) Don't talk religion or politics; (3) Women should be home taking care of their families, not working full time; (4) Minorities and immigrants are suspect; (5) Everyone gives 110 percent to the job, and that means working 100 hours a week; (6)You don't report your boss's inappropriate behavior if you want to get ahead in this organization; (7) Only men make good managers; (8) Men will be men, so allow them their jokes and jibes; (9) Don't hire anyone over 35; and (10) Gays are not welcome.

The "Good Ole Boys" Network

Many important business decisions, strategies, and advancements are made in meetings outside of formal workplace settings. "Good Ole Boys" often network by holding important business discussions or making important business decisions in such places as the golf course, the cocktail lounge, or the club, which in the past have excluded women and minorities.

General Resistance and Lack of Commitment to Change

People and the organizations they work for create habits from repeated behaviors. Disturbing these set behavioral patterns causes discomfort and resistance. Before change can take place, the individual or organization must recognize the clear benefits that will result from disturbing the status quo.

Many companies lack tangible standards and have no stated policies against discrimination and harassment. Without a clear policy statement that prohibits discrimination and harassment behaviors, malpractice continues unheeded within a traditional male workplace and becomes part of the unwritten mores of the organization.

Many companies lack a clear commitment to basic human rights. For a human rights movement to be taken seriously, company leaders must demonstrate their commitment through their day-to-day actions. They must hold themselves accountable and see that their employees are accountable for all discrimination and harassment behaviors in the workplace.

Outside Pressures

Outside pressures add to the complexity of this workplace dilemma. Business decision makers face multiple pressures, many emanating from outside the organization:

- A rapidly changing global economy;
- Massive immigration around the world and into the Americas;
- Increased discrimination and harassment litigation;
- Downsizing, mergers, and divestitures;
- Government regulations;
- Changing demographics, both nationally and globally;
- Gender, racial, and ethnic issues; and
- An explosion of new technology and data.

Massive media attention to human rights malpractice heightens tension in the workplace. The workplace dilemma is further complicated by the role society plays. All of the forces pressuring society and organizations play their part in the thoughts, emotions, and behaviors of employees. Developing effective training programs that produce significant change in the behaviors of those who discriminate against and harass others is a complicated and challenging problem and brings us to the solution to the workplace dilemma.

CHANGE THE FOCUS

Implementing the solution to the workplace dilemma means facing the fact that diversity training in its current form is the wrong solution. We believe that professionals and trainers must move their focus from an obsessive emphasis on group differences and sensitive psychological issues to a greater emphasis on similarities, tangible workplace policies and standards, and basic common relationship skills. For the purpose of this book, we term these common professional skills, Workplace Relationship Skills which are the essential core skills needed for people to work together more effectively and productively in a diverse workforce.

When we concentrate too heavily on our differences, rather than our skills, we forget how similar we are. Instead of unifying efforts, we polarize them. "The idea that whole groups or classes are victims rob individuals of an independent spirit," said Clarence Thomas in a speech to the Federalist Society. He went on to say, "Our culture's preoccupation with grouping victims has balkanized society." [14] It breeds social conflict and calls into question the moral authority of society. The grouping of victims used in diversity training programs has proven counterproductive to organizations. It has caused great unrest and backlash.

Similarly, the late Arthur Ashe, in his autobiography *Days of Grace* wrote: "I see nothing inconsistent between being proud of oneself and one's ancestors and, at the same time, seeing oneself as first and foremost a member of the common-wealth of humanity. The commonwealth of all races and creeds. My potential is more than can be expressed within the bounds of my race or ethnic identity. My humanity, in common with all of God's children, gives the greater flight to the full range of my possibilities. If I had one last wish, I would ask that all Americans could see themselves that way, past the barbed-wire fence of race and color. We are the weaker for these divisions and the stronger when we can transcend them." [15]

It is now time to stop the politics of difference, the marketing of disadvantage, the search for enemies. It is time to work on what may be the most important problem we face today—how to heal our crisis of community and together make our world work—not for blacks or whites or women or gays, not for ethnic groups or for Christians, Moslems or Jews, but for the betterment of humanity. [16]

ELIMINATE THE USE OF THE TERM "DIVERSITY TRAINING"

Because diversity training elicits such sensitive and divisive reactions from workers who would rather be treated as individuals than mistreated or mislabeled as part of a group, we recommend eliminating the use of the term *diversity* in labeling workforce training programs. Many potential participants, in seeing training sessions with the diversity label become resistant, are unwilling to participate fully, and even refuse to attend the sessions. These programs are viewed as another example of gross cultural victimization and exploitation.

The terminology associated with diversity lacks consistency and precision in meaning and use. People often use terms like diversity, culture, multicultural, and ethnicity interchangeably. Furthermore, diversity-related terms often serve as or are perceived to be euphemisms. For example, diversity is often perceived as another term for affirmative action. Similarly, some individuals utilize diversity to refer to race and gender issues, which in turn really means minorities and women.

Other workforce training programs that offer needed social skill building tools have become more fully integrated, and therefore use more effective labeling, such as: Team Building, Empowering Employees to Give Their Best, How to Communicate With "The Other," Conflict Resolution and Negotiation, How to Work With Difficult People, What to Do About Sexual Harassment, Giving and Receiving Criticism, and Business Etiquette and Professionalism. Training programs so labeled are popular with employees who want to increase their skills and become more valuable to their organizations.

Current experts and practitioners in the field of diversity anticipate that over the next few years the type of sociological changes that diversity training was attempting to instill will be integrated into other kinds of training and activities, rather than handled as a separate topic. We concur and point out that diversity training has isolated rather than integrated itself, which has been a key factor contributing toward its failure. A number of these experts also recommend a greater emphasis on specific interpersonal skill building and more focus on accountability, productivity, and competitive business needs rather than concentrating on differences. This window into the future has helped us formulate and offer this solution.

COURSE CORRECTION

To eliminate discrimination and harassment in the workplace, the following corrective steps are needed:

Stop the Denial

Discrimination and harassment practices exist inside all companies. We must stop the denial. These malpractices are behavior patterns deeply ingrained within our social culture and, as a result, have become a part of our organization's cultures. These illegal and counterproductive behaviors are acted out against targeted individuals and groups through refusal of employment, lack of promotions, limiting opportunities, sexual intimidation, and even violence.

Remove the Diversity Label

Diversity training is a failed solution for eliminating discrimination and harassment; therefore, remove the red flag. Many participants, upon seeing training sessions labeled "diversity training" refuse to attend or fully participate.

Focus on Behavior

Employers need to focus their attention and training programs on effective workplace behaviors. The diversity training focus that asks employees to change their personal value systems, beliefs, and biases has failed to eliminate discrimination and harassment practices in the workplace.

Commit to a Plan of Action

This action plan gives organizational leaders systemic guidelines with specific action steps and training processes to eliminate discrimination and harassment practices within their companies. Three components of this plan are:

Establish and Enforce a Zero Tolerance Policy for Discrimination and Harassment Practices: Organizations cannot mandate what their employees believe and value, but they can set a policy in place which makes their employees accountable for their unacceptable workplace behaviors.

Develop and Publish Company-wide Workplace Behavior Standards: Identify and educate all employees about specific acceptable and unacceptable behaviors.

Establish a Workplace Relationship Skills Training Program: Give all employees training to move toward mastery level workplace relationship skills. Assist them with skills to work effectively and productively with all employees, regardless of their differences.

SUMMARY

The complex issues of finding a solution to discrimination and harassment practices create a workplace dilemma. Costing organizations billions of dollars in training and litigation fees, diversity training failed as a solution to this dilemma. Rather than focusing on needed workplace behavior changes, diversity trainers emphasized awareness, understanding, and appreciating individual differences, thus, setting in place the demise of diversity training. The course correction needed to solve the workplace dilemma includes the following processes: Stop the denial that discrimination and harassment exist in the workplace, remove the problematic diversity training label, focus on behavior, and commit to a plan of action. This action plan includes establishing and enforcing a zero tolerance policy for discrimination and harassment practices, developing and publishing workplace standards of acceptable and unacceptable behaviors, and offering workplace relationship skills training.

NOTES

1. "Ending the Workplace Diversity Wars," Stephen Paskoff, *Training,* August 1996.

2. "Sister, Sister, What's Your Problem?" Marilyn Y. Gandy, MSW, and Joseph R. Steiner, MSW, Ph.D., *Employee Assistance,* May 1993, p. 19.

3. "You Will Feel Their Pain," Gerri Hirshey, *Gentleman's Quarterly,* March 1995, p 23.

4. U.S. Merit Systems Protection Board Report, Sexual Harassment in the Federal Workplace, October 1995.

5. "You Will Feel Their Pain," Gerri Hirshey, *Gentleman's Quarterly,* March 1995, p 29.

6. "Backlash: The Challenge of Diversity Training," Michael Mobley and Tamara Payne, *Training and Development,* December 1992, p. 46.

7. Ibid.

8. "The Quiet Race Wars," John Leland and John McCormick, *Newsweek,* April 8, 1996.

9. "You Will Feel Their Pain," Gerry Hirshey, *Gentleman's Quarterly,* March 1995, p. 215.

10. Ibid.

11. This statement was made by an executive from AT&T while attending a 1992 national summit in Seattle, Washington on diversity developed by Hellen Hemphill, Ph.D.

12. *The Diversity Machine: The Drive to Change the "White Male Workplace,"* Frederick R. Lynch, 1997, p. 172.

13. These comments were made to Hellen Hemphill, Ph.D. by a human resource executive in a Fortune 100 company in a discussion regarding diversity issues in 1994.

14. Excerpts from a 1995 speech to the Federalist Society by Clarence Thomas.

15. Excerpt from *Days of Grace,* an autobiography by Arthur Ashe, 1993.

16. Revised from the "Crisis of Comment; Making America Work for Americans," William Raspberry, *Washington Post,* April 13, 1995.

2

Harsh Realities of Discrimination and Harassment in the Workplace

INTRODUCTION

Scan the newspapers, listen to the evening news, peruse a periodical, survey the literature, talk to a friend, and you too will find example after example of organizations and individuals faced with the costly effects of discrimination and harassment in the workplace.

USX settled a class-action racial discrimination suit in 1992 for $42 million; Texaco settled a sex discrimination suit in 1991 for $17.6 million. The average cost in 1992 of an individual's discrimination suit against a company was $75,000; the cost of the average age discrimination suit was $750,000. [1]

The basic federal law against job discrimination is Title VII of the Civil Rights Act of 1964. This law makes job discrimination illegal. Employers cannot use race, skin color, age, gender, religious belief, or national origin as their basis for hiring; nor can these be used as the basis for promotions, dismissals, pay raises, benefits, assignments, leaves of absence, or any other employment relationship—from pre-hiring interviews to post-employment references.

The Civil Rights Act of 1992 broadened the law. If workers can prove that a particular employment practice tends to exclude women or minorities, for example, then the employer must show that the practice is job-related or con-sistent with business necessity.

Daily we are all confronted with a barrage of court cases indicating the magnitude of discrimination and harassment in the workplace. Recent head-lines continue to point out the scope of discrimination and harassment cases. Hundreds of articles ranging from "Boeing, Former Worker Reach Settlement in Harassment Case" to "Supreme Court Expands Scope of Law on Age Dis-crimination in Employment" have become commonplace. For the fiscal year ending September 30, 1993, a record number of job bias claims, 87,942, were filed with the Equal Employment Opportunity Commission (EEOC). The greatest number of claims was in the category of race, followed by sex, age, disability, national origin, and religion. In 1995, sexual harassment took the forefront with 15,549 cases, a significant increase from the 11,908 claims in 1993. [2] According to the U.S. Merit Systems Protection Board, between 1992 and 1994 sexual harassment in the federal workplace cost the federal government $327 million. [3]

The headlines go on and on. Cases such as the U.S. Army sexual harassment claims, the U.S. Navy Tailhook scandal, the O.J. Simpson case, the Clarence Thomas hearings, the Rodney King trial, the Mike Tyson case, and the Senator Packwood affair continue to invade the mind, the spirit, and the pocketbook of all Americans. Such cases of national magnitude have changed us socially, religiously, and politically. The cost to taxpayers runs literally to the billions of dollars. The emotional damage to our nation's citizens and their families carries a cost too large to measure.

Religious organizations often exhibit subtle and not-so-subtle discrimination practices that frequently result in hidden harassment and sexual abuse. Cases that come to public attention tarnish the credibility of church leadership, have significant monetary cost to the church body and create a negative image of the church itself. Almost never discussed is the emotional damage to the individuals involved.

Unlike cases that get national press, many stories of harassment and discrimination never make the news. These cases are not filed with the EEOC, nor do they receive the attention or compensation they deserve. This offers further evidence of the hurt and damage to both the individual and the organization.

PERSONAL STORIES

To bring your attention to the harsh realities of discrimination and harassment malpractice, we present a series of personal stories and review litigation cases covering disabilities discrimination, age discrimination, sexual harassment, race discrimination, sexual orientation discrimination, and gender discrimination.

This information provides the factual data to understand the impact of discrimination and harassment. Yet this information is only intellectual. The effects of discrimination and harassment involve both the head and the heart as the following stories will tell. They are true stories of everyday people who suffered harassment and discrimination in the workplace. They are accurate accounts of the pain and loss that invaded these individuals' lives. The names have been changed to respect individual privacy.

Dorothy's Story

Seventy-eight-year-old Dorothy Smith tells what it was like for a woman in the workplace during the 1940s. She did not use the terms discrimination or harassment as they were not and are still not a part of her vocabulary. She spoke of the isolation and confusion she experienced as one of the few women working for an international company. At that time, a married woman was not considered a valid candidate for employment; therefore, Dorothy had to keep her marriage a secret. She hid her wedding band and chose to eat lunch alone for fear that a casual luncheon conversation with another employee might risk disclosure. This could have resulted in her being fired, which in the 1940s was an accepted practice. Today, we recognize this as discrimination.

Victims of discrimination and harassment are often forced out of their jobs or take sick leave because of mental and emotional stress. Costs to the organization include: loss of individual and group productivity; decreased employee morale; increased turnover and sick leave; harassment and discrimination litigation fees; and economic and social upheaval. Families and communities suffer from human rights malpractice, as well.

Martha's Story

Martha had been employed with the same company for fourteen years. Her performance evaluations were excellent. She was promoted from a mechanical engineer, to a drafting engineer, and, finally, to a design engineer. As a design engineer, she was given responsibility for checking the preliminary designs of her co-workers. In attempting to fulfill her role as checker, she found that many of her male co-workers refused to allow her to give them feedback or professional advice. Martha also experienced gender discrimination through such sexist comments as: "Women are too much trouble;" "You don't get ahead unless you are a man;" "It's the women's fault when it isn't done right;" and "We expect to have problems when we hire a woman."

Martha told us that in order to get ahead in her company, she had to be sensitive about how she dressed and what she said in front of the men. In addition, Martha believed that her immediate supervisor was giving her easier tasks than her male counterparts, and this prevented her from demonstrating her more advanced skills. When she realized she was being passed over for promotion, Martha brought her degrees, status, and experience to the attention of higher level supervisors, but it made no significant difference.

In 1995, after designing a complex project, Martha realized that her team manager had claimed ownership of her project. Martha informed a higher level supervisor. He chose to ignore the manager's unprofessional action and did not support Martha's claim. He remarked that he had to choose his battles wisely, and this was one battle that he would not choose to fight. To Martha, this reflected a pervasive attitude of male superiority, and she chose to offer her resignation. Her department heads reviewed her resignation and explored options to persuade her to continue employment with the company. Martha was uncomfortable with the proceedings because the personnel review meeting was held in a public forum, and none of the all-male committee members made eye contact with her. The committee offered her an educational training package, with the stipulation that she would not "put the company on the carpet" if she didn't get to apply the training on the job. They closed the session with the comment that Martha should get personal counseling. She resigned.

During this time, the hostile work environment caused Martha's physical health to deteriorate. She suffered from migraine headaches, loss of sleep, and floating anxiety. Martha lost her retirement benefits, suffered serious financial difficulties, and diminished self-esteem. In the end, the company lost a valuable asset—an experienced, capable employee.

Malcolm's Story

After working for a trucking firm for thirty years, Malcolm, age sixty, was called into a meeting by his supervisor. Having received numerous awards as the company's salesperson of the year, he was expecting recognition for his usual outstanding job performance. Instead, he was told he was being let go and his position dissolved as part of a routine cutback. He was shocked. He later learned that his position was filled by a person twenty years his junior.

Malcom's self-esteem was damaged. His anger affected his family life, creating mental anguish for all. Malcolm used his retirement to start his own business. He sued the company for discrimination and settled for a significant amount. Publicity from the suit tarnished the trucking company's good image.

Catherine's Story

At age fifty-two, Catherine publicly began acknowledging her life as a lesbian. Eventually news of her sexual orientation became known to her male ecclesiastical supervisor. His response was to reorganize the department she directed in such a way that her position was eliminated. Catherine settled her suit against the church leadership out of court. She received a small litigation compensation. Six years later, she is still feeling the financial setback from the loss of her income.

Disclosure of her sexual orientation had caused her to lose her job, thus ending her exemplary, highly successful career of twenty-five years. The credibility she had achieved over the years had been challenged. The expertise and experience she had acquired was lost to her organization. No longer was there the familiar framework of the workplace in which she could utilize her skills and talents. Her history and investment of time and money went by the wayside.

DISABILITIES DISCRIMINATION

An individual with a disability is a person who has a physical or mental impairment that substantially limits one or more major life activities. Title I of the Americans with Disabilities Act of 1990 (ADA), which took effect on July 26, 1992, prohibits private employers, state and local governments, employment agencies, and labor unions from discriminating against qualified individuals with disabilities in job application procedures, hiring, firing, advancement, compensation, job training, and in other terms, conditions and privileges of employment.

For many years, our definition of disability has been limited to what is visible—such as blindness, the use of a hearing device, or a wheelchair. Today, we are beginning to recognize invisible disabilities such as HIV infection, AIDS, cancer, diabetes, and mental and emotional illnesses. We recognize the challenge these disabilities bring to both the employer and the employee.

U.S. Labor Department research identifies that there are approximately 43 million Americans with disabilities. Of this number, approximately 14.6 million are in the workforce age grouping from sixteen to sixty-five. Twenty-nine percent are in the workforce; many are part-time. [4]

Despite some positive changes in the workplace and laws passed protecting the rights of persons with disabilities, harassment and discrimination continue against them. Such barriers prevent the successful employment of disabled, yet competent persons. The following two cases are a reaction to this problem.

Disabilities Act Verdict Sends Shock Waves Through U.S. Business. In 1993, the first verdict from the Americans with Disabilities Act (ADA) stunned U.S. businesses. In Chicago, a federal court jury awarded Charles Wessel $572,000 in compensatory and punitive damages for job discrimination. Wessel was an executive who was fired when he reported his terminal cancer diagnosis to his supervisors. This landmark case demonstrated that the federal government would enforce the ADA laws. This suit is a good example of attitude discrimination that the ADA was designed to correct. It demonstrates the fear and myths of disabilities. [5]

EEOC Files Suit Against Employer that Fired HIV Positive Truck Driver. In the second case, a San Francisco trucking firm violated the Americans with Disabilities Act (ADA) by firing a driver who had tested HIV positive, the virus that causes AIDS. The Equal Employment Opportunity Commission (EEOC) filed a suit against the trucking company in the federal district court. The EEOC's suit alleged that the company willfully violated the ADA principles by firing and then refusing to reinstate the driver. The driver asked for punitive damages of $100,000 for failure to re-employ, compensatory damages, back pay, and emotional suffering. [6]

AGE DISCRIMINATION

Workers between the ages of forty and seventy are protected by the Age Discrimination in Employment Act (ADEA), which was passed in 1967 and amended in both 1978 and 1986. The law applies to all private employers who employ twenty or more workers and to federal, state, and local governments, employment agencies and labor organizations made up of twenty-five or more members.

Statistics indicate that older employees use fewer sick days, stay with their employers longer, and have fewer on-site accidents than younger workers. When these facts are taken into consideration, it is obvious that older workers become increasingly valuable in maintaining a productive economy. Yet, in spite of this, discrimination continues.

Demographics show that the "graying workforce" is aging dramatically. The Bureau of Labor Statistics projects 39 percent of the labor pool will be forty-five or older within the next decade, up from the current 31 percent. It is estimated that by the year 2000 there will be 38 million employees over age forty-five, but only 34 million employees in their twenties. The low birth rate from 1964 to 1974 resulted in a drastic decline in the number of young workers from six-teen to twenty-four who would make up that entry level workforce. Because of this, demographers predict a shortage of young, entry-level workers by the late 1990s.

In 1981, there were no fewer than 9,500 charges of age discrimination filed with the EEOC. As of 1994, the number of age-related cases climbed to 17,009. A report by Jury Verdict Research, a legal publishing firm in Horsham, Pennsylvania, reveals that plaintiffs fired because of age bias are awarded much higher damages than people fired because of race, sex, or disability. Successful age bias claims resulted in average awards of $302,914, compared with awards of $255,734 for sex discrimination, $176,578 for race discrimination, and $151,421 for disability discrimination. [7] The median of all awards showed even larger gaps between age cases and discrimination cases. The following cases and settlements give us a small glimpse into the scope and impact of age discrimination on the individual and the organization:

Pan American World Airways Settled In Age Discrimination Suit—$17.2 Million. In 1988, the EEOC pursued a suit on behalf of pilots challenging Pan American World Airways' practice of terminating pilots at age sixty and not allowing them to transfer to other positions in the company. This resulted in a settlement of $17.2 million. [8]

Jury Awards $1 Million For Age Claim Against New York City Aging Department. A federal jury returned a $1 million verdict in 1995 against the New York City Department for the Aging and its former commissioner for violating age discrimination laws. The department discharged sixty-one-year-old Joyce Stratton, who had been director of the Central Information Department for fifteen years. Stratton lost her salary, benefits, and hundreds of hours of sick leave. Compensatory damages of $500,000 were doubled to $1 million because the jury found the violations to be willful. [9]

Shaw vs. HCA Health Services of Midwest, Inc. Thomas Shaw, director of the radiology department in Doctor's Hospital in Little Rock, Arkansas, from 1975 to 1993, was fired. He sued the hospital in federal court, alleging age discrimination. Mr. Shaw's compensatory damages of $125,600, liquidating damages of $125,600, and back pay of $550,000 totaled $801,200. [10]

Maiorino vs. Schering-Plough Corporation. In 1991, Ferdinand Maiorino, a former sales representative for the Schering-Plough claimed that he had been fired because of his age. A superior court judge in New Jersey awarded $8.42 million to Mr. Maiorino. [11]

$28 Million Awarded to a 65-year-old Man. An award of $28 million was given in 1992 to a sixty-five-year-old man who charged a subsidiary of Consolidated Freightways with age discrimination. The *San Francisco Chronicle* cited this as one of the largest awards in the U.S. in age discrimination suits. [12]

SEXUAL HARASSMENT

In a 1994 study, the federal government estimated the cost of turnover among federal employees due to sexual harassment at approximately $24.7 million during a one-year period. Adding the cost of sick leave and the loss of individual and work group productivity elevates that figure to a projected $327.1 million. This does not include the effect of this harassment on the victims.

Even if no threat is intended, unwelcome sexual conduct toward another person is defined as sexual harassment and can have the effect of "poisoning" a victim's work environment. Sexual harassment was first recognized as illegal discrimination in 1977 and upheld by the Supreme Court in 1986.

Data submitted to the Equal Employment Opportunity Commission headquarters by EEOC field offices and state and local Fair Employment Practices Agencies (FEPA) show a dramatic increase in sexual harassment cases from 1990 to 1995. In 1990, 6,126 cases were filed with the EEOC. By 1995, the number had reached 15,549. The monetary benefits awarded in 1995 were $24.3 million.

In the landmark 1986 decision in *Meritor Savings Bank vs. Vinson*, the U.S. Supreme Court ruled that sexual harassment occurs whenever any unwanted sexually oriented behavior changes an employee's working conditions and creates a hostile or abusive work environment, regardless of the level of economic loss for the victim. [13] This decision has since been reinforced and redefined by the courts and organizations in a government-wide study by the U.S. Merit System Protection Board. [14]

Other landmark events such as the Clarence Thomas and Anita Hill congressional hearings, the U.S. Army sexual harassment cases, and the U.S. Navy Tailhook scandal alerted all Americans to the abuse and sexual harassment of women and left women much more aware of their rights. While society today appears to be more sensitive to the issues of sexual harassment, the problem has by no means disappeared. Both men and women continue to be sexually harassed in the workplace.

Since passage of a 1992 law allowing damages of as much as $300,000 per person in certain job discrimination cases, the number of job bias cases filed by private law firms has shot from 8,140 in 1991 to 19,059 in 1995. Of the total number of cases in 1992, 132 charges of sexual harassment were filed by male employees. This number increased to 412 in 1994. One example is Douglas Hartman's nationally reviewed case. He reported that he was sexually harassed while attending a company-sponsored diversity training workshop for his employer, the Federal Aviation Administration. He stated that "female hands skimmed his thighs and brushed his genitals, and voices cried, 'Nice Buns!' " This was an activity called the "gauntlet," a reverse of the U.S. Navy Tailhook scandal process. Hartman filed a federal lawsuit under Title VII of the Civil Rights Act and received the maximum amount of $300,000, plus legal costs and payment of medical bills for stress-related ailments for both his wife and himself. [15]

A 1996 study by the Department of Defense indicated that incidents of sexual harassment are reported in five broad categories: (1) crude offensive behavior—e.g., unwanted sexual jokes, stories, whistling, staring; (2) sexist behavior—e.g., insulting, offensive, and condescending attitudes based on the gender of the person; (3) unwanted sexual attention—e.g., unwanted touching, fondling; asking for dates even though rebuffed; (4) sexual coercion—e.g., classic *quid pro quo* instances of job benefits or losses conditioned on sexual cooperation; and (5) sexual assault—e.g., unsuccessful attempts at and having sex without the respondent's consent and against his or her will.

The following cases give further evidence of the astronomical cost to companies who do not protect their employees from sexual harassment:

Jean Jew vs. University of Iowa. The university was ordered to pay a female professor a total of $1,070,000—$50,000 in back pay, $125,000 in damages, and $895,000 in fees and expenses—ending a five-year court battle. The university's president also publicly apologized to the professor. [16]

Jury Awards $50 Million In Wal-Mart Harassment Suit. In a sexual harassment suit against Wal-Mart, a federal district court jury in 1995 awarded

$50 million in punitive damages to Peggy Kimzey of Warsaw, Missouri. She also received $35,000 in damages for humiliation and mental anguish and $1 million for lost wages. Wal-Mart is appealing. [17]

Jury Awards Over $8 Million In Damages To Worker In Tyson Foods Processing Plant.   An Alabama federal jury in 1993 awarded $8 million in punitive damages to a Tyson Foods chicken processing plant worker. Tyson was found guilty of maintaining a sexually hostile work environment. Emotional distress and invasion of privacy were cited. [18]

Del Laboratories Agrees To Record Sum For Settling Sexual Harassment Lawsuit.   In 1995, Del Laboratories, Inc. agreed to the largest sexual harassment settlement in U.S. history. A federal court judge ruled that Del should pay $1.2 million to the 15 women who claimed they were harassed by Dan K. Wassong, chief executive officer, president and chairman of the Farmingdale, New York, cosmetics company. The EEOC's lawsuit accused Wassong of engaging in lewd behavior and using vulgar language in the presence of female employees. [19]

Five Million Dollar Lawsuit Accuses College President Of Harassment.   In 1995, Marilyn Marshall, a former administrator of Paul Quinn College, filed a $5 million lawsuit that accused President Lee E. Monroe of sexually harassing her and then firing her for not submitting to his advances. She claimed that Monroe propositioned her and asked her to travel with him to Mexico. When she refused, he demoted her to a position at the college's now defunct campus in Waco, Texas. [20]

Grim Tales from the Gardens: The Sex Scandal at the Hockey Mecca Keeps Growing. "For years victims kept the Garden's secret. But in January 1997, a Toronto native, Martin Kruze, 34, became the first to blow the whistle, leading to the arrests of Stuckless, 47, and John Paul Roby, 54, a part-time usher for 25 years. Both were charged with gross indecency and indecent assault." [21]

Pierce County Medical Examiner Fired Amid Sex Charges, Scandal—Damages Could Exceed $500,000. Dr. Emmanuel Lacsina, Pierce County, Washington, medical examiner, was charged in May 1996 with perpetuating a "sexually charged workplace." Two other claims for damages are pending, both charging discrimination and retaliation; each seeking the amount of damages that could exceed $500,000. [22]

RACE DISCRIMINATION

Under Title VII of the Civil Rights Act, race discrimination is illegal. Race discrimination affects all those who significantly differ in color and culture from the dominant white male class in U.S. businesses. This includes African Americans, Asian Americans, Hispanics, Jews, Native Americans, recent immigrants, and all others who are not of white European descent.   These racial groupings often occupy a subordinate power position in society and in the U.S. workplace. "Racial disparities continue to persist," points out Andrew Hacher in his 1992 book, *Two Nations: Black and White, Separate, Hostile, Unequal.* [23]

The largest number of complaints filed with the EEOC involve race discrimination and according to the EEOC report for the years 1990 to 1994, that number continues to climb. In 1990, 29,159 cases of race discrimination were registered with the EEOC. By 1994, the number had climbed to 31,656.

The following examples give evidence of the negative effects of race discrimination in the workplace:

Kim vs. Nash Finch Company. In 1995, a federal jury in Cedar Rapids, Iowa awarded a Korean American employee $8.79 million in damages for race discrimination and retaliation by Nash Finch Co., the nation's fifth largest grocery wholesaler. The employee claims that Nash Finch refused to promote him because of his race and national origin. The claimant was awarded an additional $1.75 million for emotional injuries and $7 million for punitive damages. [24]

California Jury Awards Over $4 Million To Three Coca-Cola Co. Employees in Promotion Case. A state superior court jury in 1996 awarded more than $4 million in damages to two black drivers at a Coca-Cola distributor. They sued Coca-Cola for failing to promote them because of their race. One of the plaintiffs, Tyrone Douthered, was frequently referred to as "nigger" and passed over for promotion thirty-one times because of his race. Because his emotional distress was intentionally inflicted, he was awarded $986,000 in compensatory damages and $900,000 in punitive damages. [25]

Circuit City Charged With Bias In Suits Filed By Black Employees. In a case that is still pending, eighteen former and current employees have filed two suits in federal court against Circuit City Stores Inc., charging unlawful discrimination against black employees and hiring procedures that discriminate against black people. The plaintiffs allege that Circuit City engages in a deliberate, systematic and continuing practice of denying equal compensation, promotion, and transfer opportunities to qualified African American employees. The claim states that the company treats African American employees more harshly than similarly situated white employees and disciplines, demotes and terminates black workers at a disproportionate rate. [26]

$24.5 Million Awarded To 273 Railroad Employees. Twenty-seven years of legal battles came to an end in 1993 with a court settlement that awarded $24.5 million to 273 current and former African American railroad employees. Seventy-three former train porters and 200 former chair-car attendants sued their employer, Santa Fe Railway and the United Transportation Union for racial discrimination and sought damages commensurate with the wages they lost by being barred from whites-only jobs. [27]

New Suits Filed Against Denny's Restaurant. Kousar Bhutto, a Pakistani, and Mirnezam Massouleh, an Iranian, filed suits in 1995, seeking $4 million for having to endure a hostile work environment and discriminatory and degrading acts. This pending suit states that class action status will be requested for damages of $4 million. [28]

SEXUAL ORIENTATION DISCRIMINATION

During 1993 Senate hearings on the issue of gays in the military, Senator Sam Nunn offered the following solution: "We won't ask any questions, and you don't give any answers." His intention was to ensure that sexually diverse men and women would remain invisible. His remarks echo the tacit agreement of mainstream society to require that lesbian, gay, and bisexual individuals not disclose their sexual orientation. This creates individuals who live on the edge of disaster, never knowing if or when their disclosure will bring harassment or discrimination. Silence becomes a way of life. They remain hidden and are forced to live a lie.

In *The Celluloid Closet,* author Vito Russo says that, "The big lie about lesbians and gay men is that we do not exist. . . . America is a dream that has no room for the existence of homosexuals." This position is strengthened by the fact that from 1990 to 1994, there were no statistics reported by the U.S. Equal Employment Opportunity Commission on sexual orientation discrimination in the workplace. [29]

Workforce researchers have not focused on the *gay question*; and therefore, little data is available about the discrimination against persons who are lesbian or gay. Individual cases seldom move to litigation because most states and municipalities do not recognize sexual orientation as a category against which discrimination is banned. Since there are no federal laws prohibiting discrimination based on sexual orientation, discrimination significantly continues but goes largely unrecorded. For example, Title VII of the Civil Rights Act of 1964 does not include sexual orientation as a protected class, which means that we do not have a body of evidence to prove that this type of harassment or discrimination exists.

The *Cracker Barrel* incident is an example of this lack of protection. In 1993, this fast-food chain fired eleven employees because they were either lesbian or gay. Their new corporate policy stated that "homosexual employees are incompatible with traditional family values." The New York City Pension Fund, one of several shareholders, protested this discriminating policy and called for a boycott. Despite national attention to the case, the company remained intractable. The New York Pension Fund divested itself of all Cracker Barrel stock. The fired employees had no recourse under state or federal law. They either remained unemployed or found jobs elsewhere and eventually had to give up the case. [30]

Currently, only nine states have passed some form of legislation designed to protect lesbians and gays from discrimination and harassment. They are: Wisconsin (1982), Massachusetts (1989), Hawaii (1990), New Jersey (1990), Connecticut (1991), Vermont (1991), California (1992), Minnesota (1992), and Rhode Island (1995).

Some existing data on employment discrimination against gays and lesbians is beginning to emerge from such sources as individual complaints brought into court or before state human rights agencies, surveys done by civil rights organizations on employment discrimination and widely gathering evidence of violence and harassment directed at people because of their sexual orientation.

Surveys done by nearly a dozen civil rights organizations reveal that gays and lesbians report high levels of workplace discrimination. Data indicate that many gay and lesbian people reported being fired when their sexual orientation was disclosed. Sexual and violent harassment and unfair work practices were frequently reported. Gays and lesbians were routinely passed over for promotions, job upgrades, and pay raises.

In 1992, the General Accounting Office (GAO) reported the dollar cost of governmental discrimination against gays and lesbians. Because of the military's anti-gay policy, fourteen hundred military personnel who had been trained for specific jobs were eliminated each year from 1980 through 1991. All were trained for specific jobs and had to be retrained for other careers at military expense. The expense of retraining did not include the cost of investigations. The GAO estimated the cost of the investigation for 1990 alone exceeded $2.5 million.

The ruling of the Supreme Court on May 20, 1996, handed gay rights advocates their biggest legal victory to date in making unconstitutional an amendment to the Colorado constitution that forbade laws protecting homosexuals from discrimination. This will not end the negative effects of discrimination and harassment of homosexual minorities in the workplace, but it does offer an avenue of recourse to the legal system that will alert employers and employees to stop harassment and discrimination of sexually diverse employees. The following cases offer insight into the negative effects of such harassment and discrimination.

California Court Awards $5.3 Million in Damages for Termination of a Homosexual.   Jeffrey Collins had been employed for nineteen years as a manager at a biotechnology company in California. He was earning $115,000 a year when a simple oversight—leaving a copy of a "safe sex" gay invitation in the photocopy room—cost him his job. Angry and humiliated for being forced to accept a job at a pet-shipping company for one-fifth the salary he had been making, he filed a discrimination suit. He won a record $5.3 million. [31]

Lesbian Sues Over Ouster after a Twenty-Seven-Year Military Career.   A decorated Vietnam veteran, Margarethe (Greta) Cammermeyer, was drummed out of the National Guard because she is lesbian. On her last day in uniform she vowed she would fight the Pentagon's order to cut short her military career of twenty-six years. On June 1, 1994, Cammermeyer won her case. In a fifty-page ruling, Judge Thomas Zilly of the federal district court in Seattle wrote that Cammermeyer had been discharged under a regulation "based solely on prejudice." "Prejudice, whether founded on substantiated fears, cultural myths, stereotypes or erroneous assumptions, cannot be the basis of discriminatory classification," he said. "There must never be a military exception to the Constitution." [32]

GENDER DISCRIMINATION

If you are a woman and/or a member of an ethnic, religious, or racial minority, you are part of a protected class as defined by Title VII. It is ironic that members of Congress, when debating this historic piece of legislation, added "discrimination on the basis of sex" as a device to defeat Title VII's strong protection of minorities. Title VII now stands as the most comprehensive law protecting the rights of women and minorities, and prohibits discrimination based on race, color, sex, religion, or national origin in these areas:

- Hiring, including recruitment and testing;
- Wages and benefits;
- Promotions, transfers, layoffs, and recalls;
- Firing;
- Training and apprenticeship programs;
- Assignment and classification of employees; and
- Working conditions.

The 1963 Equal Pay Act makes wage discrimination based on gender illegal. Title VII was amended in 1972 to include discrimination based on gender. But just as the overall labor market remains sharply segregated by sex, so are women executives concentrated into certain types of jobs—mostly staff and support jobs that offer little opportunity for getting to the top. The "glass ceiling" for women is not simply a barrier for an individual, based on the person's inability to handle a higher level job. Rather, the glass ceiling applies to women who are kept from advancing solely because they are women.

In 1993, 31,695 gender discrimination claims were filed with the EEOC. In 1994, FEPA statistics registered 19,321 resolutions, and the EEOC registered 21,542 resolutions. In 1994, these two agencies collectively resolved 40,863 gender cases. The monetary awards resulting from litigation for gender discrimination approximated $65.8 million.

According to the *Securities Arbitration Commentator*—a Maplewood, NJ newsletter—twenty-six arbitration awards have been made during the past two years to Wall Street women alleging sexual harassment or discrimination. This is more than in all five previous years combined. [33]

The workforce of the United States is currently comprised of some 49 million people. Forty-four percent of the workforce are women. It is anticipated that by the year 2000, this number will increase to approximately 50 percent. Despite the Equal Pay Act of 1963, which requires employers to pay equal wages to men and women doing jobs calling for equal skills and equal responsibilities and under similar working conditions, full-time female employees continue to be paid less than their male counterparts.

The following cases emphasize the enormous challenges society faces today. Each case challenges assumptions and stereotypes regarding roles and rules for men and women in the workplace. These cases also cause significant financial loss to both the individual and the employer.

Collins Oil Field Maintenance vs. Shell Oil, Jury Awards Million. Female business owner Jackie Collins of Bakersfield, California, was awarded $1 million and in May 1995, the Ninth U.S. Circuit Court of Appeals upheld the court order that Shell Oil Company pay her damages for gender discrimination. Collins sued when Shell Oil Company canceled its contracts with her construction and maintenance company. In this process, a Shell foreman allegedly stated, "Women do not belong in the oil fields." When her company failed, Collins was forced to work as a waitress. [34]

Jury Awards over $5 Million in Damages to Former Executive Who Claimed Sex Bias. A jury for the U.S. District Court for the Eastern District of New York awarded plaintiff Mary Ann Luciano $5 million in punitive damages, $150,714 in back pay, $11,400 for emotional distress, and $17,713 for other damages. The employer had failed to promote Luciano and ultimately fired her because she was female. Luciano claimed that she had been denied equal terms and conditions of employment compared to similarly situated male managers. This jury award, at the time the largest ever, was held up as an example of women being held back by the invisible but inevitable glass ceiling. [35]

Court Approves Plan to Distribute Funds in $10 Million Detroit Police Settlement. A federal judge in 1995 approved a plan that called for the City of Detroit to distribute $10.8 million to 890 female officers and job applicants in settlement of a long-running sex discrimination suit against the city's police department. In their complaint, the officers claimed the department had systematically discriminated against a class of women officers and job applicants. When the suit was filed in 1973, female applicants were required to have at least two years of college to join the department, while male applicants were admitted with only high school diplomas. Female officers also were paid less than their male counterparts and lost out to male colleagues in promotions. Payments to individuals, which ranged from $71,000 to more than $96,000, are in settlement of a twenty-two-year-old federal lawsuit concerning women who either worked for or applied for jobs in the police department from 1970 to

1978. On September 26, 1995, Judge Paul Gadola of the U.S. District Court for the Eastern District of Michigan approved the distribution plan that compensates class members for lost earnings, interest, personal injury, and "impairment of reputation." [36]

Albertson's Settles Bias Suit—Agrees to Pay $29.5 Million. Albertson's, a grocery chain based in Boise, Idaho, agreed in 1993 to pay $29.5 million for lost wages and emotional stress in a race and sex discrimination case. Female employees did not get equal opportunity or training for promotions. They were given less desirable work shifts and often were placed in sex-segregated jobs. Subject to federal court approval, $4.5 million will go to the law firm handling the case for distribution. [37]

Safeway Inc. Agrees to Settle a Lawsuit on Sex Discrimination. Five million dollars was awarded in 1994 to certain female Safeway employees who were victims of sex discrimination. The company's northern California stores were accused of discrimination, which included, among other practices, segregating women into lower-paying departments such as delicatessen and bakery and maintaining low numbers of women store managers. [38]

Severe Harassment Found at Washington State University. Federal findings revealed that as a recipient of federal funds, Washington State University failed to live up to its civil rights responsibilities. The report found that a significant number of severe and harassing behaviors by male co-workers and supervisors affected the work environment of women employees. The lengthy report was a part of a class action sex discrimination complaint filed in November 1994. [39]

SUMMARY

As seen by the cases described in this chapter, the negative effects of discrimination and harassment are extensive. Companies have settled thousands of cases, at a cost of millions of dollars annually. Most of us understand money and its implications for our lives, our pocketbooks, and the well-being of our families. Money speaks for itself. Money brings to national attention the seriousness of discrimination and harassment as they affect the workplace.

But the hidden costs of discrimination are not so easily discerned. The mental anguish, the shame, and the emotional strain of fighting for one's rights cannot be measured in dollars and cents. Workforce data and statistics present a vivid picture of job turnover and sick leave. There is a probable decrease in both individual productivity and group productivity because of discrimination and harassment practices.

Even as employees become better-informed and speak out, harassment and discrimination practices will in all likelihood continue among those who still feel the need to control or choose to remain prejudiced. We cannot risk the temptation of denial and avoidance. Each of us—senior management, supervisors, and employee alike—must accept the challenge to eradicate the harsh reality of harassment and discrimination in the workplace. Failure is not an option. The cost is too great.

Discrimination and harassment hurt us all. Every incident is an abuse of power. Discrimination and harassment diminishes human potential, creates a hostile work environment, affects the bottom line, and costs millions of dollars. Each wrongdoing continues to perpetuate myths, stereotypes, and false beliefs about the skills and competence of every human being in the workplace.

As a result of continuing discrimination and harassment, companies lose out in obtaining and retaining the bright minds and talents they drastically need. Discrimination and harassment in the workplace destroys the spirit and heart of employees, erodes the quality of the workplace, and undermines our American belief in "liberty and justice for all."

NOTES

1. "Texaco's White Collar Bigots," Jack E. White, *Time,* November 18, 1996.

2. Equal Employment Opportunity figures reported throughout the text are taken from EEOC's computerized Change Data System (CDS), which is continually updated by field offices and state and local Fair Employment Practices Agencies (FEPAs) around the country.

3. Merit Systems Protection Board, Sexual Harassment in the Workplace, October 1995.

4. "43 Million Will Be Protected by Law," Ann Ryan, *USA Today,* January 1992.

5. "Disabilities Act Verdict Sends Shock Waves Through U.S. Business," *Seattle Post-Intelligencer,* May 9, 1993.

6. "Equal Employment Opportunity Commission Files Suit Against Employer That Fired HIV Positive Truck Driver," *Bureau of National Affairs Employment Discrimination Report,* 1072-1967-'95, October 23, 1995.

7. "Age Bias Cases Found to Bring Big Jury Awards," *Wall Street Journal,* December 17, 1993.

8. "Pan American World Airways Settled an Age Discrimination Suit—$17.2 Million," *Seattle Times,* February 4, 1988.

9. Jury Awards $1 Million for Age Claim Against New York City Aging Department, *Bureau of National Affairs' Employment Discrimination Report,* 1072-1977-'95, December 1, 1995.

10. "Shaw vs. HCA Health Services of Midwest, Inc.," 70 FEB Cases 464, March 18, 1996.

11. "Maiorino vs. Schering-Plough Corporation," New York Public Law Commission, November 28, 1994.

12. "28 Million Awarded to a 65-Year-Old Man," *San Francisco Chronicle,* October 10, 1992.

13. "Meritor Savings Bank vs. Vinson," Supreme Court Ruling 2406, 1986.

14. U.S. Merit Systems Protection Board, Sexual Harassment in the Workplace, October 1995.

15. "You Will Feel Their Pain," Gerry Hirshey, *Gentleman's Quarterly,* 1995, p. 215.

16. "Jean Jew vs. University of Iowa," *City Press Citizen*, November 9, 1990.

17. "Jury Awards $50 Million in Wal-Mart Harassment Suit," *Wall Street Journal*, June 13, 1995. In December 1995, these punitive damages for harassment were reduced to $5 million.

18. "Jury Awards Over $8 Million in Damages to Worker in Tyson Foods Processing Plant," *Wall Street Journal*, July 21, 1993.

19. "Del Laboratories Agrees to Record Sum for Settling Sexual Harassment Lawsuit," *Wall Street Journal*, August 4, 1995.

20. "Five Million Dollar Lawsuit Accuses College President of Harassment," *The Chronicle of Higher Education*, November 10, 1995.

21. "Grim Tales from the Gardens," Tom Fennell, Canada: *Macleans*, March 10, 1997.

22. "Pierce County Medical Examiner Fired Amid Sex Charges, Scandal—Damages Could Exceed $500,000," *Seattle Times*, May 28, 1996.

23. *Two Nations: Black, White, Separate, Hostile, Unequal*, Andrew Hacker, 1992.

24. "Kim vs. Nash Finch Company," *Bureau of National Affairs Employment Discrimination Report*, 1072-1992-'96, March 8, 1995.

25. "California Jury Awards Over $4 Million to Three Coca-Cola Company Employees In Promotion Case," *Bureau of National Affairs Employment Discrimination Report*, 1072-1967-'95, October 31, 1995.

26. "Circuit City Charged with Bias in Suits Filed by Black Employees," *Bureau of National Affairs, Employment Discrimination Report*, 1072-1967-'95, October 31, 1995.

27. "$24.5 Million Awarded to 273 Railroad Employees," *Seattle Times*, July 19, 1993.

28. "New Suits Filed Against Denny's Restaurant," *Seattle Times*, November 12, 1995.

29. *The Celluloid Closet*, Vito Russo, 1987.

30. "Cracker Barrel, New York City Pension Fund," *New York Times*, April 10, 1993.

31. "California Court Awards $5.3 Million in Damages for Termination of a Homosexual," *San Francisco Chronicle*, June 10, 1991.

32. "Lesbian Sues Over Ouster After a 27-Year Military Career," *Associated Press*, July 6, 1992.

33. "The Wall Street Fails to Stem Rising Claims of Sex Harassment and Discrimination," *Wall Street Journal*, May 24, 1992.

34. "Collins Oil Field Maintenance vs. Shell Oil, Jury Awards Millions," *The National Law Journal*, Vol. 16, No. 17 & 18, December 27, 1993.

35. "Jury Awards over $5 Million in Damages to Former Executive Who Claimed Sex Bias," *Bureau of National Affairs Employment Discrimination Report* 1072-1962-'95, November 9, 1995.

36. "Court Approves Plan to Distribute Funds in $10 Million Detroit Police Settlement," *Bureau of National Affairs Employment Discrimination Report*, 1072-1967-'95, September 26, 1995.

37. "Albertson's Settles Bias Suit—Agrees to Pay $29.5 Million," *Wall Street Journal*, November 23, 1993.

38. "Safeway Inc. Agrees to Settle A Lawsuit on Sex Discrimination," *Wall Street Journal*, April 4, 1994.

39. "Severe Harassment Found at Washington State University," *Seattle Times*, May 7, 1996.

3

Society's Role in Perpetuating
Human Rights Malpractice

INTRODUCTION

America's working population is multicultural. A mixture of races and ethnic groups is the rule, not the exception. Yet the discrimination and harassment against targeted outsiders continue. The ongoing theme of diversity in American politics and American industry has not changed since its beginning; all that has changed are those discriminated against.

In the late 1800s and early 1900s, immigrants from countries such as Poland, Italy, Ireland, and Russia were considered inferior because of their cultural backgrounds, religious affiliations, ways of thinking, and difficulties with the language. Slowly, these groups gained collective economic clout and established their place in the business world. Because women from these ethnic groups did not work outside the home, that clout was both white and male. Discrimination remained rampant toward and among them. Protestants and Catholics discriminated against each other, and they both discriminated against those of the Jewish faith. Over a sixty-year span, the integration of white males of various ethnic and religious groups gradually took place. Collectively, they became the white-oriented male population that forms the establishment in American commerce today. [1]

As women of all races and racial minorities entered the workplace, their advancement was blunted by labor and management's discriminatory practices. Dennis Dickerson, author of *Out of the Crucible: Black Steelworkers in Western Pennsylvania*, states that what happened to black steelworkers at the beginning of the Depression in the 1930s is perhaps the greatest proof that the exclusion of blacks had little to do with issues of merit and competition and everything to do with race. Dickerson reports that steel mills commonly employed black steelworkers to train newly recruited white workers. After training was completed, the mills then gave white workers the blacks' jobs and laid off the black workers. [2]

In that time, white ethnic immigrants needed to ally with other groups just as today minority groups need the support of competent management who understand what is happening.

Now, however, the picture is changed. Daily, the media deluge us with information. In fact, so many books, screenplays, and television scripts are being written that it is hard, except on a global scale, to understand the divergence of viewpoints that underscore the worldwide practice of discrimination and harassment. Through repetitive stories from people of highly diverse origins, the full extent and truth of this problem has been revealed. Only through the accurate telling and interpretation of humanity's story on a global scale does the spectrum of human rights malpractice become clear.

Advanced technology allows us to access stories worldwide, a phenomenon which has inevitably reshaped our values. Racial upheaval, sexual revolution, change in the balance of power between men and women, and loss of a positive national identity have left their mark. This, in its broader relationship to the transformation of American culture, has a profound and direct effect on business.

Fifty years ago, Americans had traditional values that were based on social discipline. Divorce was a disgrace, as was welfare. Authority was vested in men as breadwinners and heads of the household. Most men did not permit their wives to work. Nonwhites remained quietly invisible. Homosexuals were called perverts. Millions had never heard of lesbians.

Fifty years ago Americans stood for duty and country. Today, each American is willing to fight for his or her individual rights—civil rights, women's rights, children's rights, gay rights, white men's rights, welfare rights, adoption rights, animal rights, the right to life, the right to choose, the right to protest, the rights of the disabled. Anything that infringes upon personal territory in any way whatsoever is now considered worth fighting for. Individual freedom has become more important than individual responsibility. This is reason enough for the radical change in how Americans view themselves and one another.

THE REVOLUTION OF CHANGING RIGHTS

The prime mover in transforming America's social values is the medium of television. Prime-time TV brings the world into our living room, leading viewers to stand as eyewitnesses to unwed, lost, and disillusioned teenage mothers, rampant and pillaging teenage gangs, or subterfuge in the White House. Mass media will continue to be a platform for change. One cannot watch the dramatic shifts in our sexual behavior, discrimination and harassment of women, reverse discrimination, political upheaval and corruption, cultural differences, man's inhumanity to man, and the changing roles of men and women and not change oneself. Just as we are subtly or profoundly moved by extraordinary acts of love and valor, we are just as subtly or profoundly changed by all we see. The mind's eye cannot differentiate between reality, a dream sequence, or something on the big screen. We are changed, each one of us, by all that comes across our perceptual field, whether or not we choose to recognize and acknowledge that change.

U.S. business is increasingly sympathetic to this change in American culture and, in particular, how each person views individual rights. A Fortune 500 chief executive officer relates, "We used to have a lot of white male traditions. We bought season tickets to sporting events, and we called the annual management outing President's Golf Day. Our first two women officers complained. They didn't play golf or follow the Yankees. We realized these activities were no longer appropriate. They were too male-oriented and unwittingly made females feel like outsiders. We were unintentionally sending a message to women and minorities that said, 'Welcome, come inside, but be like us.' Now we no longer buy season sports tickets; we do buy tickets to the ballet and symphony and have memberships in museums. And we've changed the name of our outing to President's Day and widened the choice of activities to include jogging, tennis, swimming, or just lying by the pool." [3]

Other companies have followed this line of action. With this in mind, we now focus on three primary groups: those involving women's rights, white men's rights, and minority rights. In particular, we explore how women, white men, and minority populations have been affected by new rules that have been superimposed on and—thereby change—former roles and relationships in America's workplace.

WOMEN'S RIGHTS

Prior to World War II, male and female roles were more clearly defined. But as men went off to war, women shifted from their accepted life-roles as caretakers of the home into that of service providers in the previously male-dominated workplace. Women functioned as heads of households in their husbands' absence and became competent performers in office and industry. Many women who were fortunate enough to have their men return home from war chose to remain in the workforce; those not so fortunate had no choice and forever altered American history. Yet today, fifty years later, many men still believe that woman's only place is in the home, an attitude that while often unexpressed, continues to permeate the work world and hold women back. Because of this basic attitude, many men remain untouched by social change around them, allowing discrimination against women in the workplace to continue. Harassment of women who choose to stay on to become part of the American workforce remains a serious problem.

Female writers involved in the Women's Liberation Movement brought gender inequities to the world's attention. Liberated women believed they were held back solely because of their gender from developing appropriate skills to compete with men for good jobs in the workplace. These women educated themselves, joined the mainstream workforce, and demanded an end to gender discrimination everywhere. Before the sexual revolution of the sixties, comprehensive literature concerning women and their treatment in the work world was almost nonexistent. Thanks to women who battled, fought, and won, such literature can no longer be avoided. Neither can the discrimination issues it has raised.

Dr. Philomena Essed of the University of Amsterdam interviewed fifty-five black women from both the Netherlands and the United States for her study on racism to understand the profoundly subtle discrimination they experience daily. This ten-year-long project resulted in her book, *Everyday Racism,* which revealed that there is an unquestionable amount of ongoing experience of racism in the lives of these women. [4]

Women will make up about 61 percent of entrants into the U.S. workforce between 1985 and 2000. Moreover, women's participation in the workforce will continue to grow; by the year 2000, 47 percent of the workforce will be women, and 61 percent of women will be employed. [5]

A key component in the transition of women into the world of work is their educational prowess. Women now constitute 49 per cent of all undergraduate students. Today, more women than men are likely to complete their degrees and graduate. For example, during the decade when medical schools stopped discriminating against women, the schools didn't change their admissions criteria; they just dropped the traditional quota system that had restricted the number of female medical students to no more than seven percent. During those years, the average class shifted from seven to 47 percent female, proving essentially that, given the chance, women compete and women excel. [6]

The proportion of women receiving master's degrees in business administration jumped from four percent in 1972 to nearly 35 percent in the early 1990s, representing nearly a ninefold increase. Women now receive approximately 44 percent of all doctorates awarded to U.S. citizens. That number was a mere 19 percent in 1973. For the first time in history, women are more likely than men to seek all major types of advanced degrees, which includes master's and doctorates as well as those in medicine or law. [7]

According to the Trendwatch column in *Executive Female,* enormous changes have taken place in the past few decades:

- In 1968, woman left work for ten years after her children were born; in 1987, leaves of absence changed to six months. Figures for 1996 are not yet available, but anecdotal evidence suggests the average leave could now be as low as six weeks.

- In the last nine years, the number of workers employed by women-owned firms has nearly tripled from 6.6 million to an estimated 18.5 million people in 1996.

In 1986, women earned sixty-four cents for every dollar earned by men. Because of job discrimination, college-educated women averaged fifty-five cents for every dollar of salary earned by men with the same academic credentials. Women who broke into management and administration still earn an average of 50 percent of the earnings attributed to men holding these same positions. [8]

In another article from *Executive Female*, a different story emerges. According to a recent survey of 1,269 graduates of top-tier business schools, the average starting salary of female MBAs ($69,642) now exceeds that of males ($69,227). [9] The survey, conducted by the Fuqua School of Business at Duke University, also revealed that before enrolling in business school, the men had been earning an average of 21 percent more than the women ($48,705 vs. $40,813). [10]

Notwithstanding the increase in female educational stature, senior executive and board of directors' positions are still filled by males at least 95 percent of the time. Women and minorities make up only three percent of the executive force in the top 1,000 companies in America. In the top 2,000 corporations, the number of women and minorities in top executive positions moves up to five percent. The *Wall Street Journal* reports that these figures are misleading because they are based on the study of Fortune 1000 companies. [11] However, a 1995 statistical abstract of the United States demographics reveals that 48.4 percent of all management jobs and 52.8 percent of all professional jobs are held by women. [12]

Behind the emergence of the American female was a slowly developing political movement. It was fueled not only by the demanding voice of American feminists, but by a growing number of men who believed that inequities against women should be halted. Despite the passing of the Equal Pay Act of 1963, gender discrimination had little emphasis in federal legislation until the Title VII addendum to the Civil Rights Act of 1964, which dealt with employment discrimination. With this new legislation, strong federal laws and regulations enforced nondiscrimination on the basis of race, color, religion, gender, and national origin.

The end of discriminating behavior against women in the workplace was supposed to occur when ineffectual state laws protecting women rights became void if they conflicted with the federal mandate for equal employment opportunity for both sexes. That is to say, federal law supersedes state law. Yet, in the workplace, where the action is taking place, discrimination and harassment still persist.

Three highly significant developments affected the national move toward eliminating discrimination of women and minorities in business:

1. *Supreme Court Decision*: In 1971, the U.S. Supreme Court unanimously endorsed a definition of employment discrimination under Title VII of the Civil Rights Act of 1964. The Court indicated that intent is not enough; it is the consequences of an employer's actions that determine whether or not the action may have been discriminatory. An employer must justify any action that has an adverse effect on the employment status or opportunity of women and/or other minorities.
2. *Administrative Order*: In 1972, an administrative order was issued by the Office of Federal Contract Compliance, which required government contractors to have a written affirmative action plan for each of their establishments, including goals and a timetable for use in a good-faith effort to increase the representation of women and minorities in all job categories where they were currently underutilized.
3. *Consent Decree*: In 1973, the American Telephone and Telegraph Company (AT&T) signed a multimillion-dollar consent agreement with both the Equal Employment Opportunity Commission, the government entity which administers Title VII Law, and the Department of Labor, the government entity which administers the executive order. AT&T agreed to take affirmative action steps to provide equal employment opportunities for minorities, which included women. The cost to AT&T was estimated at close to $100 million over a five-year period. [13]

These mandates forcefully put U.S. corporations on notice. In short, eliminating discrimination and harassment was no longer an opinion; it was the law. As employers and government contractors, corporations had significant nondiscriminatory obligations to women, as well as to other minorities. The federal government, backed by the federal courts, mandated that women be allowed equal opportunity in the corporate structure; consequently, the most impacted corporations responded by hiring women.

Yet, despite unprecedented numbers of women in the workplace and their presence in management ranks; and despite an international women's movement and its proliferation of women's concerns in the media; and despite radical modernization of many societies, men and women are still treated differently. In almost all situations, men and women are talked to and talked about differently. They are touched differently, and approached differently. They are addressed and dealt with through role assumptions and expectations held over from what should by now be a bygone era. To this day, the treatment of women remains significantly different than the treatment of men, something that once upon a time might have been brushed aside as a simple fact of life but is today a state or a federal offense, punishable by law, for which taxpayers are paying millions. This is a bottom line issue for both businesses and individuals. [14]

Recent management studies reveal that women are more poorly paid, less frequently promoted, and given less time to speak at meetings. When allowed to speak, their voice is not heard. Women receive less useful feedback on their performance, and often are assigned to domestic duties in the workplace as well. [15]

With federal legislation and the stronger stance taken by the federal courts to protect women's rights, discrimination and harassment litigation has become a serious threat to U.S. companies. As mentioned earlier, women have won thousands of discrimination and harassment suits against their employers. This assault on the bottom line of corporations has worked as a catalyst forcing many organizational leaders to focus their attention and financial resources on solving discrimination and harassment of targeted groups or individuals. It is sad to say that the bottom line, rather than human decency, is more often than not the prime mover in this equation, but that is the truth of the matter.

Diversity training, with its ascribed special treatment for women and minorities, laid the groundwork for the demise of many of the affirmative action programs of the 1970s and 1980s. Legislation which threatens the future of women's rights is still pending. The Equal Opportunity Act of 1995, H.R. 2128, is an anti-affirmative action bill. It would cause a number of changes in laws relating to women and minorities and wipe out three decades of bipartisan federal civil rights enforcement policies. It would eliminate all effective federal affirmative action programs and jeopardize equal opportunity for women and minorities. As of this writing, the 97th U.S. Congress was considering six anti-affirmative action bills aimed at eliminating programs for women and minorities. On another frontier, in November 1996, California passed Initiative 209, the California Civil Rights Initiative (CCRI), which rolled back the clock on affirmative action that bans racial and sexual preferences in public hiring, contracting, and education. "The actual effects of affirmative action are reported as quite modest, in spite of the fact that it has been blamed for many things, including hiring of unqualified people and shutting white employees out of jobs," states Jonathan S. Leanard, professor of organizational behavior at University of California at Berkeley Haas School of Business. [16]

Federally backed programs, however, have given women the opportunity to prove that they are capable of being excellent employees and to demonstrate that they have management and leadership capabilities. Women have entered the marketplace and will continue to compete for the good jobs. Regardless of pending legislation, women in the workplace are here to stay.

Not everyone agrees that legislation is solely responsible for the advancement of the cause of women. An alternative view discredits affirmative action programs and suggests, instead, that the status of women has improved more from cultural change and from enforcing nondiscrimination than by preferential treatment. According to economist June O'Neill, in the nearly thirty years since affirmative action programs were introduced, women have done quite well. Women between twenty-seven and thirty-three, who don't take time out for child-rearing now earn 98 percent of that earned by men. Women as a group presently earn more than $1 trillion a year. They own almost 6.5 million businesses. They employ 35 percent more people in the U.S. than Fortune 500 companies do worldwide. Nearly 42 percent of all households with assets of over $600,000 are headed by women. [17]

Ms. Ellen Ladowsky, a Washington-based journalist, states that the final undoing of affirmative action was actually endorsed by women. A *Washington Post* poll stated that 69 percent of white women and 76 percent of men oppose affirmative action. Nonworking women, or women temporarily out of the workforce raising children, count on their husband's salaries and promotions to support their families. Too often, it is the husbands, brothers, or sons of these women who have been the victims of affirmative action's reverse discrimination. [18]

The erasure of the blatant distinctions between men and women has made the most dramatic change of our time. It has helped and hurt both men and women alike. It is not surprising there is backlash from those whose power has been taken away. But the fact that this backlash has swung around to hurt the very people affirmative action was trying to help, speaks of deeper issues yet to come.

WHITE MALE RIGHTS

White males cry reverse discrimination as their rights are violated and they become unseated. Women and minorities now receive those special privileges they are used to, and this poses a serious threat not only to the economy but also to the emotional well-being of the workforce. According to Catherine Crier of ABC-TV, white males believe that a caste society has been created, one in which there are two classes of citizens: those who are protected by civil rights laws and those—themselves—who are not. [19] Many men believe that when racial imbalance became proof of discrimination through government-backed quotas, white males were deprived of the protection against discrimination that the Civil Rights Act provided women and minorities. According to the *Seattle Times*, six cases have been reported nationally in which white male employees won successful individual claims proving they were discriminated against in favor of minorities and women. [20]

Diversity trainer Larry Baytos compiled the following list of nine questions. These questions regarding diversity programs were raised by dozens of participants in focus groups made up of white males with white male leaders.

- Why is the company doing this diversity stuff at this particular time? Don't we have enough on our plate already?
- Isn't diversity just another name for affirmative action in the kinder, gentler 90s?
- Isn't affirmative action just a code word for quotas and compromising our hiring standards?
- With downsizing and re-engineering, there aren't enough opportunities in our company as it is. Won't the diversity program simply further reduce the opportunities for white males?

- Affirmative action got them in the door, and now diversity will move them up in the organization. But what's in it for me? Why should I become a supporter of the diversity program?
- If diversity is so important, why is the senior management of this company composed almost entirely of white males?
- I am fearful of going to diversity awareness training (or whatever the company calls it). Will it just be a lot of white male bashing? I don't think I should take the blame for all of society's ills. This company is not exactly a picnic for me to work in either!
- As a white male, what can I do to help? Are my input and my participation really welcome, or is this something for women and minorities to do the work on with the human resource department? [21]

"Almost to a man, they are furious," says Warren Farrell, a San Diego-based therapist who conducts workshops on men's issues and author of *Why Men are the Way They Are.* "They feel it on a personal level. They feel it's condescending to women and minorities, and it has undermined the country's ability to compete globally." Farrell goes on to say that the majority of the men attending his workshops say they have seen less-qualified women and minorities get the promotions that passed them by. They also claim women and minorities abuse the system by taking more time off, calling in sick more often, and refusing to work graveyard shift or accepting a transfer. White men admit that they dominate the top echelon, but the vast majority of men never make it that high. Instead, they languish in middle management, which is precisely where women and minorities have made the most progress. At that level and below, white men feel they are at a distinct disadvantage. [22] They can no longer languish, they must now compete.

Just a few years ago, white men complained bitterly to themselves and to pollsters that competition from women and minorities was imperiling their career climb and job security. Opposition to affirmative action among white men surged from 44 percent in 1992 to 67 percent in 1995. It appears, however, that the anger is cooling off. According to the 1996 poll, opposition to affirmative action among white men has dropped to 52 percent. [23]

What has caused this drastic change in opposition to affirmative action? It appears that the rise of women and minorities in some companies has slowed or even halted. Under the ruse of keeping their employees happy, companies are soft-pedaling or scaling back diversity programs in response to white-male backlash. A changing political climate, including recent Supreme Court decisions limiting the use of affirmative action in education, is convincing many white men that the high-water mark of affirmative action has passed. To many white men this seems a return to fairness. But to many women and minorities, it is a step backward that imperils the slim progress made in recent decades. "White men will continue to get the lion's share of the benefits," says Greg Jeffries, a black real estate developer with Citylands Corp., a subsidiary of

Shorebank Corp. "When the economy heads south they'll look for scapegoats and blame women and minorities once again." [24]

The men's movement, perhaps best represented by poet Robert Bly in his book *Iron John* is attempting to redefine the world of work. Bly says, "Today's male leaders mourn the loss of fathers they never got to know because their jobs—not their families—were the center of their lives. Men are hurting, they say—isolated, lonely, engaged in cutthroat competition at work." Bly describes the male mystique: Men don't need a connection to family or community. They don't fatigue as easily as women. They're unemotional, rational, power-driven, highly competitive and "capable of machine-line efficiency" at work. They have come to be associated with the machines they operated. [25]

Men are expected to be rational and non-emotional. In many organizations this has been translated into the concept of "Just tell me what you think and keep your damn feelings to yourself!" While men have the power, they pay the price with a 10 percent shorter life span than that of women. Furthermore, men now represent 70 percent of alcoholics, 70 percent of drug addicts, 70 to 80 percent of suicides, and 80 to 90 percent of the homeless.

Joseph Potts, director and president of the National Training Laboratories Institute, and himself a white male, states that white men have been unconsciously socialized in ways that allow them to avoid dealing with emotionally loaded issues. He says that it would take an exceptional set of events to motivate them to take action towards ameliorating racism and sexism in our organizations—most of all because they are unconsciously a part of it. The business climate may provide sufficient motivation to explore issues of oppression, but it is not an adequate stimulus to take serious action. Men are very uncomfortable dealing with issues that they cannot solve, and they do not know how to solve this issue. White men receive mixed messages. Intellectually they might believe in equality, but emotionally they have been taught that they are the best. Many white men have been raised to believe that women are "less than" men. Potts reports witnessing many men deliberately treating women as inferior to men as part of this ingrained, cultural teaching. [26]

The changes taking place in the workforce and in the new employer/employee work covenants of the 1990s is hitting the white man hard. Today's white males, especially those with only a high school education or less, feel less secure economically than their father did—although they might want to reconsider thinking that the job they wanted has somehow been handed over to a black person or a woman in the name of affirmative action. Gone are the days of the gold watch. Gone are the days when lateral moves were sudden death to upward mobility. Both lateral moving and downward mobility has become the norm, not the exception. And in the changing sphere of that corporate America, it is more likely that the job in question is now located in Taiwan or Singapore, or that it has gone up in the smoke of corporate mergers and downsizing.

Being traditionally male, acting masculine, being the "manly" man in the downsizing organization have become a potential liability. According to surveys by Mark Maier, author of *Glass Ceilings: Glass Prisons* the "best managers" are not obsessed with maintaining authority—they empower others. They do not simply focus on getting the job done, they care about how the goal is achieved. Best managers support and develop employees, they respect and listen to them, and they care about their employees' needs and interests. Not only are they goal-oriented, efficient, and responsible, but they are also communicative, personable, understanding, and open to suggestions. [27]

This is not a description of the traditional "manly" man in American culture. Nor is it typical of what was once thought to be a "good manager" in the American workplace, bringing to focus the effect women have had on the workplace. The glass ceiling remains, but the climate is changing.

Maier goes on to suggest that men want the same rights that women want. Companies like Mobil, DuPont, Corning, Merck, IBM, and Johnson & Johnson report that internal audits of their managers show that men not only want to have families, but that they want to be involved with them. In a poll conducted in 1989 by Robert Half International, 56 percent of the men surveyed said they would give up as much as one-fourth of their salary to have more family or personal time; 45 percent indicated they would probably refuse a promotion that involved sacrificing hours with their family. Historically speaking, this has been considered the woman's view and the woman's problem. Successful managerial men were supposed to marry and father children but act like they were single.

In traditional corporate cultures, it is not acceptable for men to acknowledge their need for family involvement, despite the lip-service paid to so-called "family men." Even the current debate over child care and the provisions corporations are making to assist working parents with their mutual parental responsibilities are only surface considerations. Child care is still seen as a gender issue. Most businesses aim only at protecting organizational investments in women as "human resources" rather than seeing the overall picture by helping both male and female employees be more involved with their families. The continuum has been disturbed, but the wheel is not completely turned. [28]

MINORITY RIGHTS

For the first time in history, in the 1996 Presidential elections, a winning campaign ticket had as part of its platform a plea for the elimination of discrimination and harassment of minority populations in the U.S. The Clinton/Gore ticket called for the rights of all to be considered so diverse groups can come together to cross the bridge into the twenty-first century. U.S. companies must consider the rights of their diverse minority populations. By the year 2050, one-half of the U.S. population will be African American, Hispanic

American, Native American, and Asian American. This is a pool from which companies must select their future workforce. It will also be the makeup of their future customers. New entrants in the U.S. labor force by the year 2000 are projected to be primarily composed of minority groupings: Asian females, three percent; Asian males, three percent; black females, seven percent; black males, six percent; Hispanic females, seven percent; Hispanic males, eight percent; white females, 35 percent, and white males, 32 percent. In fact, white males will also become a minority population. [29]

This mix of races and ethnicity is fueled by the immigration of minority groups from all over the world. Almost nine million immigrants arrived just during the 1980s. That means that 43.8 percent of America's 19.8 million foreign-born population came in the 1980s. Those who arrived in that decade were overwhelmingly Hispanic and Asian. Immigrants are about eight percent of the total U.S. population today. [30]

In spite of its diversity, America has never been free of ethnic and racial bigotry. Discrimination against the black population has been historically the most fertile ground for such bigotry. In spite of the Emancipation Proclamation of the 1860s that freed American slaves and the governmental laws and mandates crafted since to eliminate discrimination, the subordination of the African American (and other minority populations) continues. In 1963, President Kennedy urged Congress to pass further civil rights legislation to combat discrimination against blacks. His address to Congress stated, "One hundred years have passed since President Lincoln freed the slaves, yet their heirs, their grandsons, are not fully free. They are not yet freed from the bonds of injustice. They are not yet freed from social and economic oppression. And this nation will not be fully free until all its citizens are free." [31]

More than thirty years later, discrimination is still widespread against people of color. Through education and the protection of U.S. laws and government mandates, the rights of minorities have increased. Affirmative action and equal employment opportunity laws have opened the doors for the mandated inclusion of minority populations in companies using government contracts. Minority employees composed about 12 percent of the workforce in the 1960s. They were primarily hired in staff positions—one-third of African American employees are in middle-class occupations. However, according to a survey by Korn/Ferry International, an executive recruiting firm, minority representation totaled less than one percent in senior level jobs. [32]

Diversity training came into practice to help organizations deal with the influx of minorities (including women) and the application of affirmative action laws and equal employment opportunity practices. Minorities were allowed into the corporate pipelines, but little has been done to get them into top jobs. Efforts continue through such organizations as the U.S. Labor Department Office of Federal Contract Compliance Programs. Under the Glass Ceiling Initiative (GCI), federal compliance officers will focus for the first time on examining succession plans in corporations—how individuals are selected for key high-level corporate positions. [33]

Until the landmark 1989 lawsuit filed against Shoney's of Pensacola, Florida, Shoney officials held to a system-wide unwritten policy of refusing to hire blacks.   This turned into what was then the largest class action racial discrimination suit in U.S. history.   Shoney was required to pay $15 million to between 75,000 to 80,000 of their minority employees.   Shoney additionally agreed to invest $92 million over a three-year period in minority-owned franchises.   It also named several people of color to executive positions.   As a part of the settlement of this suit, Shoney will step up its hiring and recruiting goals for minorities and will establish an internal complaint system for black employees.   Discrimination against minorities continued to cost companies millions of dollars through the '90s. [34]

SUMMARY

Similar to many U.S. companies, Texaco is being confronted with more discrimination lawsuits in 1996.   Company executives were taped openly discussing shredding minutes of meetings and other documents that would incriminate them in discrimination suits filed by black employees.   These tapes bolster the charges that Texaco discriminated against minorities in promotions and fostered a racially hostile corporate environment.   They also show that Texaco did not learn from past experience with earlier discrimination suits.   In one such suit settled in 1991, Texaco paid a record $17.7 million in compensatory and punitive damages to Janella Sue Martin, who sued for sex discrimination after the company denied her a long-promised promotion and gave the job to a man instead.   Another pending suit involves six black employees who are suing Texaco for alleged race discrimination.   They have asked a federal court to impose sanctions against Texaco for its alleged failure to produce documents. [35]

The transcripts from the 1996 Texaco case offer a rare and revealing glimpse into the bigotry and hypocrisy that still festers at the apex of the corporate world despite three decades of affirmative action.   "Whenever we try to talk about racism, people say nobody has those views anymore, especially not polite, well-educated people," says Mary Frances Berry, chairwoman of the U.S. Commission on Civil Rights.   "They tell us it's just those poor-white-trash types who do these sorts of things."   If the Texaco tapes are any indication, biased attitudes often go all the way to the top, and the surest way to entrench them is to pretend they no longer exist." [36]

NOTES

1. "Workforce Diversity and Business," Badi G. Foster, Gerald Jackson, William E. Cross, Bailey Jackson, and Rita Hardiman, *Training and Development,* April 1988.

2. *Out of the Crucible: Black Steelworkers in Western Pennsylvania*, Dennis Dickerson, pp. 46-49.

3. "12 Companies That Do the Right Thing," *Working Women*, January 1991.

4. *Everyday Racism: Reports from Women of Two Cultures*, Philomena Essed, 1990.

5. "The Future of HRD," George F. Kimmerling, *Training & Development*, June 1989, p. 46.

6. "Global Conference in Managing Diversity," AIMD Research Notes, Vol. 2, Issue 10, October 1995.

7. Revised from Jennifer James Column, *Seattle Times*, December 3, 1995.

8. "Enormous Change in the Last Decade," *Executive Female*, September/October 1996, p. 44.

9. "Trendwatch," *Executive Female*, October, 1992, p. 7; "Women MBAs Earn More," *Executive Female*, September/October 1996, p. 43.

10. "Reports of Our Conquests Were Highly Exaggerated," *Executive Female*, May/June 1996, p. 27.

11. "Misleading Figures," *Wall Street Journal*, March 27, 1995.

12. *Statistical Abstract of the United States in 1995*, U.S. Department of Commerce, Table 649, p. 411.

13. *The Upward Mobility of Senior Management Females in the 1980s*, doctoral thesis, Hellen Hemphill, Ph.D., Saybrook Research Institute, 1989.

14. Revised from "The Ultimate Cultural Difference and How to Bridge It," *Careers & Engineers*, April 1995, p. 32.

15. "The Downside of Diversity," Victor C. Thomas, *Training and Development*, January 1994, p.60.

16. "Berkeley Professor Sees No Economic Erosion for Whites and Modest Effect for Blacks," *The Chronicle of Higher Education*, November 17, 1995, p. 64.

17. Smith Barney Bulletin, Fall 1996.

18 "Undoing of Affirmative Action," *Washington Post*, February 3, 1993.

19. Address by Catherine Crier, ABC-TV *20/20*, November 18, 1994.

20. "Reverse Bias Against White Men Not a Big Problem," *Seattle Times*, April 1, 1995.

21. Larry Baytos, president of Diversity Implementation Group, listed questions males asked in group work. The Diversity Training Library Newsletter and Catalog, Vol. 1, No. 1, Winter, 1996.

22. "White Men and Managing Diversity," Marilyn Y. Gandy, MSW, and Joseph R. Steiner, MSW, Ph.D., *The Diversity Factor*, Spring 1993, p. 14.

23. "That is No White Male," *Wall Street Journal*, March 27, 1995.

24. "Fixing Affirmative Action," Mortimer B. Zuckerman, *U.S. News & World Report*, March 20, 1995.

25. *Iron John*, Robert Bly, 1990.

26. "Can White Men Help?" Kate Kirkham, *The Diversity Factor*, Spring 1993, p. 22.

27. "Glass Ceilings, Glass Prisons: Reflections of the Gender Barrier," Mark Maier, *The Diversity Factor*, Spring 1994, p. 17.

28. Ibid.

29. U.S. Department of Labor Bulletin, 1992.

30. "Immigrant Tide Surges in '80s," Margaret Usdansky, *USA Today,* May 29, 1992.

31. President Kennedy supported the passage of human rights legislation in his congressional address, January, 1963.

32. "OFCCP launches 'glass ceiling' initiative," Bureau of National Affairs, "The Challenge of Diversity: Equal Employment Opportunity and Managing Difference in the 1990s," p 23.

33. Ibid

34. "Shoney Settles Race-Bias Lawsuits," *USA Today,* November 6, 1992.

35. "$105 Million Settlement in Bias Case Puts Business on Notice," *USA Today,* February 14, 1993.

36. "Texaco's White Collar Bigots," Jack E. White, *Time,* November 18, 1996.

4

The Diversity Training Movement and Its Failure

INTRODUCTION

The underlying expectation of the diversity training process was to provide an avenue of learning and create a level of awareness that would eliminate discrimination and harassment in the workplace. At first, diversity training seemed to be the needed answer and, over time, it developed a following. To update what happened in the movement and why, we first discussed the predicaments facing society, organizations, and individuals in the workplace. As these scenarios played out, much to the dismay of those purchasing the training and those receiving it, diversity training failed to diminish discrimination and harassment behaviors in the workplace. We believe the reason diversity training has failed to provide the much-needed answers is because its central focus places attention on ideas and ideologies rather than on behaviors and skills.

THE DIVERSITY TRAINING MOVEMENT

When a *Workforce 2000 Report* used the term "diversity" in 1987, it soon became a buzzword. The report predicted that before the turn of the century, 84 percent of the entry-level workforce would be made up of females and minorities. Among the startling projections were the following: White males would account for only 15 percent of the 25 million people who joined the workforce between the years 1985 and 2000. The remaining 85 percent would consist of white females, immigrants, and minorities (of both genders) of black, Hispanic, and Asian origins. [1] Many business leaders were convinced that they must prepare their companies and employees for the enormity of these demographic changes, and so the stage was set for the development of diversity departments and the creation of diversity training programs. It is interesting to note that a printing error indicated that non-Hispanic white males entering the workforce would drop to 15 percent from 47 percent by the end of the century. Recent U.S. Bureau of Labor Statistics forecasts indicate that non-Hispanic white males will decrease by only three percentage points between 1994 and 2005, to 38 percent from 41 percent. The error was caught and the information corrected, but the erroneous information is still believed and cited. [2]

The Civil Rights Act of 1964 provided laws that ensured fairness to all individuals in the workplace, with the exception of gays and lesbians. As a result, terms like equal employment opportunity and affirmative action entered the business lexicon. Human resource departments were given the responsibility of ensuring compliance with these laws. Training programs were designed to raise the level of awareness regarding gender and minority issues in the workplace. It was hoped that creating awareness would engender understanding and thereby eliminate discrimination and harassment practices in the workplace.

By 1996, female and minority employees accounted for more than one-half of the U.S. workforce. In spite of this ongoing demographic shift, the attitudes and values of (predominantly white) males still, consciously or unconsciously, dominate today's workforce. This domination was recognized by diversity training programs which by 1991 began to focus on sensitizing the white American male. Their purpose was to help white males develop more acceptable and creative ways of working with female and minority subordinates. The focus on enlightening white males, however, was only one of a wide range of reasons that companies continued to support diversity training programs. Diversity trainers Allison Rossett and Terry Bickham offer additional reasons:

- *Compliance*: "The Taxpayers expect us to do something." "Our Shareholders expect us to do something." "If we get sued for racial or sexual discrimination, at least we'll be able to point to the diversity classes we offered."
- *Harmony*: "We want our people to get along—to understand and appreciate one another."
- *Inclusion*: "We want under-represented employees to achieve success in this organization." "We want to help majority employees work successfully with diverse colleagues."
- *Justice*: "We have to acknowledge it. There has been inequity here and our employees need to understand that." "We're part of a larger effort to right past wrongs."
- *Transformation*: "We want to make certain we've all thought long and hard about what new and diverse employees, customers, and markets mean to our organization." "This is all part of a process that will change the way this organization does business. It might even mean changing our core values, processes, and standards." [3]

Companies joined the diversity bandwagon for many reasons, but mainly because their competition did. Companies were wooed by such consultants as Lewis Griggs and Lennie Copeland, who, in 1987, produced the first best-selling diversity training videotape, "Valuing Diversity," which combined a humanistic and business agenda. [4] In 1990, R. Roosevelt Thomas authored a *Harvard Business Review* article ascribing a stronger business orientation for managing diversity. [5] All of these early leaders fostered the premise that workplace diversity was good for business.

Diversity training programs emphasize various other needs, such as managing differences or avoiding lawsuits. Although most diversity training programs are designed to comply with affirmative action regulations, selecting a general program without matching it to the particular needs of the individual company proved counterproductive and only complicated the problem. [6]

In a 1991 survey of 406 companies, The U.S. Conference Board found that more than 60 percent of U.S. companies with one hundred or more employees had diversity training programs and more were planning to implement such programs. [7] In spite of the increased interest in diversity programs, diversity administrators typically worked with severely limited budgets. In addition, national guidelines for diversity curricula and trainers were all but non-existent; thus companies had no early base on which to formulate strategic planning. However, in 1996, the American Society for Training and Development (ASTD) published the first consolidated diversity training work entitled, "The Elements of Competence for Diversity Work," which drew on the experience of many of the nationally known authors. [8]

DIVERSITY TRAINING MYTHS

Myths, simply put, are the beliefs of a people. They can accrue around a person, a phenomenon or an institution. They are most often not proven. They may be true, they may not be true. What matters most is that they are believed.

As with any societal movement, myths or beliefs have arisen around aspects of diversity. One example of a diversity myth is the idea that one race is superior to another. The errors in *The Workforce 2000 Report* became a media myth. Here are more:

Minorities and women are the most-qualified to deliver diversity training to white males, but white males are not qualified to speak for women and minorities. The biased thinking that women and minorities are the only ones qualified to lead diversity training programs is a type of prejudice, believes Darlene Seidschlaw, director of EEO and affirmative action compliance at US WEST in Denver. She states, "All trainers have to uncover their own prejudices before they can work on the prejudices of others." Training programs that do not include white males in their development and training roles increase fear and resistance among white males and eventually harm the organization's efforts to reduce discrimination and harassment, sowing the seeds of white male backlash. David Tulin of Tulin DiversiTeam Associates, a diversity training consulting firm in New York City, was quoted in a 1993 article as saying, "You end up with radically different expectations. This increases the minorities' anger and frustration and increases the white male's isolation and exclusionary behavior." [9] It also exposes both the male problem and the white male problem within the company power structure.

Diversity training is effective. Diversity training may give the impression that a company has dealt with diversity, when in reality the glass ceiling and discrimination and harassment remain intact. Ineffective diversity training can raise false expectations of women and minorities. It increases fear and resistance among minority males, who are held back, and white males, whose security is threatened. It can harm the organization's effort to find solutions to the workplace dilemma. Some diversity trainers encourage people to discuss things in a group that they would not otherwise talk about and that later has been used as ammunition against them. Companies have been sued and forced to pay heavy fines for comments made by trainers and employees in diversity training programs. Employees who were exposed to painful exercises in which emotions and feelings that had been kept dormant became activated were sent back to the workplace without the corporate infrastructure needed to support the changes taking place in them and their surroundings. This is a bit like creating a loose cannon; no one knows what will happen and consequently no one knows how to behave.

Without strategies in place to support it, diversity training usually fails. Poor training practices can give the wrong clues about what to do in any given situation, such as reacting by simply not hiring white males. The pain that comes from dealing with personal prejudice in a diversity training program can intimidate both the employees and employers and make them reluctant to take part further in diversity training sessions. Many companies sandwich diversity training between other workplace programs, such as team building and quality improvement, without giving any thought to the importance of developing a comprehensive workplace policy to manage differences or consider diversity training's impact on these other training programs.

Diversity is about race and gender. Focusing on the narrow scope of race and gender only served to alienate workers further and led to diversity training's inevitable failure. A broader definition of diversity is "all the ways we are different." This would include such things as age, education, training, socioeconomic status, culture, gender, race, sexual orientation, religion, military experience, and ethnicity.

The workforce needs to become more "politically correct" in the use of language about diverse collectives. In order to be productive workers, employees need to feel respected. That means that in order to be politically correct, we must completely eliminate domineering, discounting, name-calling, harassing, discriminating, or maligning behavior in all forms. Yet some people see political correctness as a direct threat to their First Amendment rights. The PC movement has, in fact, created a legal and social minefield. People confuse such terms as political correctness, diversity, multiculturalism, pluralism, equal employment opportunity, and affirmative action. They walk around on egg-shells, afraid that if they make a mistake, their good intentions will not be recognized, or that intentions will be read into their actions that otherwise were not there. [10]

Targeting men's negative and inappropriate attitudes toward women and minorities will help increase the equality of communication between men and women and between men and minorities. Fostering any form of an "us versus them" environment makes victims of us all. Training conducted by women and minorities has often appeared to beat up on men. This has instilled fear, bred resentment, and caused an inevitable backlash that has come not just from white men but from white women too.

Glenn Rifkin writes, "If we want to diversify successfully we must help not only minorities but also white males with their adjustment to the workplace. If we don't, white males will disengage, and we will not get the benefits everyone hoped for from diversity." [11]

Myths that no longer hold true, or are not workable in today's workforce, lead to unnecessary misunderstandings. It is important for each one of us to uncover our own prejudices before we can work on the prejudices of others. It is imperative for each of us to evaluate our own values, biases, and prejudices in order to remove diversity myths from our work relationships.

A DEEPLY FLAWED APPROACH

"Most diversity programs share a deeply flawed approach," state diversity trainers H.P. Karp and Nancy Sutton. "Finger pointing, white-male bashing, language policing. They're just some of the ways to kill a good idea." [12]

From Karp and Sutton's work come these observations:

- Because of the assumption that men will not understand the minority point of view, trainers are usually women or ethnic minorities.
- The emphasis is on sensitizing the white male manager, because he is the one who caused the problem and needs to do most of the changing.
- The programs usually reflect a specific set of values, with an emphasis on changing people's attitudes, rather than dealing with their behaviors.
- Diversity awareness is the sole theme of the program; thus the program is not focused on real-life activities, nor is it integrated into other company training programs or policies.
- Programs are frequently guilt-driven and contain endless examples of grave injustices done by one group to another. This tends to polarize the different groups into victims and oppressors, which increases resentment among the groups rather than reducing it.
- How a thing is said gains more importance than what is said or intended. Attention to language can be overdone and, again, can create more problems than it solves.

Most diversity trainers focus on the past and/or the future. Little attention is paid to what is happening in the organization right now or how to develop the skills to deal with it.

HOSTILE BACKLASH

Companies originally viewed diversity training as a form of soft revolution, a way to produce a team-oriented, flexible organization. Consequently, diversity training has been on the rise for the past ten years. So has the backlash caused by the many issues it has surfaced. Most companies had no way of anticipating that backlash. Nor were diversity trainers prepared when they were blamed for creating backlash because of the cultural elements they had unearthed.

In 1992, John Leo, a nationally syndicated columnist, warned that organizations that bring in diversity consultants "think they are buying social peace, when they are more likely to be purchasing social conflict." Conflict between dominant and minority groups, brought to the forefront by diversity trainers, sowed the seed of counterrevolution. [13]

If the purpose of this soft revolution was to form a sensitive and efficient workforce from the existing social mix, it has not been successful. It is evident that diversity training programs have not alleviated social oppression in the workplace. Raising individual consciousness concerning prejudice, discrimination, and harassment has not been effective in creating organizational change. Nor have diversity training interventions altered organizational power structures and their dominant culture. Training courses meant to bring people together deteriorated into personal agenda-venting sessions or merely dissipated. Too often the best intentions have been polarized by political correctness. In the worst case scenarios after diversity training interventions, seemingly well-run companies have become units of dissension.

Unfortunately, presenters often proved to be aggressive, hostile, and combative. Confrontation training practices in diversity training courses that focused on historical abuses against gender, race, and ethnic groups only brought deeply rooted prejudices to the surface. Left without an avenue for healing, these freshly opened wounds merely festered. As a result, even the word diversity now brings to mind negative and fearful feelings to many. The original intent of diversity training was to eradicate prejudices that kept women and minorities from succeeding in business. Instead, diversity awareness training was most often conducted by women and minorities, and mostly focused on targeting white men. In the early nineties, the media began to write front page articles about this phenomenon. In 1992, *The San Francisco Chronicle* ran a story that stated, "Elsie Cross is a 62-year-old black woman who is in the business of changing white men. And a big business it is." [14]

Many people came to believe that the point of diversity training was to change white men. The result was an emerging counterrevolution, a direct retaliation to the diversity training that first targeted white men's attitudes toward women and minorities and that has been covertly festering for years.

Since the early 1990s, media articles have repeatedly brought diversity training into question. A 1995 *Washington Post* article brought to national attention just how serious male backlash had become. [15] That same year, male backlash acted as a catalyst for a national political movement against affirmative action and diversity. This movement successfully eradicated a portion of earlier government-mandated support for equal employment opportunity for women and minorities. There is national media speculation that this outrage is just beginning to be felt. Diversity training activities such as the following are credited with fueling the nationwide backlash:

- Diversity trainers who directly confront their participants, demanding that within their group setting, the participants expose their personal bias, whereas prior to this exposure their personal bias was not shown through their behavior;
- Women and minority trainers who use diversity training sessions as a forum for their own hostile personal agendas; and
- Trainers who target white males as a primary cause of prejudice, bias and discrimination issues.

Frederick R. Lynch, in *The Diversity Machine,* described diversity trainers' desires to discuss cultural differences and yet avoid negative group stereotypes as the diversity paradox. [16] Diversity trainers, intent on solving the complex problems that cause oppression and discrimination within organizations, stirred the pot but did not solve the problem.

The magnitude of the problems facing diversity trainers was greatly underestimated. Organizations abetted trainers in fostering diversity training's failure by giving it lip service and responding only superficially. Most organizations did not realign their internal structure to bring about long-lasting systemic change. Since organizational rules that dominated or created the culture went unwritten, a glass ceiling remained and free discussion was limited. Personality issues, feelings, personal values, religious beliefs, political differences, and sexual orientation issues that arose were not in appropriate context within the U.S. workplace.

Today, lack of job security and radically changing employment conditions place diversity issues in an even worse pressure cooker. Increased competition for limited resources causes many corporate decision-makers to make difficult judgments—such as the release or retention of difficult employees or employees that do not fit the status quo—in ways that are not in compliance with human rights goals. Race and gender issues have become a political hotbed. With the downsizing or right-sizing of white managers, reverse discrimination has become a war cry.

Employee fears are compounded by the reaction of men, young and old, to the perceived opinion that white males are responsible for every ill. The prideful superiority that the white American male has had in being white, American, and male is now threatened. [17]

"The 'white male workplaces' that diversity consultants wish to restructure may harbor varying degrees of ethnic and gender discrimination. But today's large-scale workplaces are primarily complex social systems of rules and goals that are also impersonal and insensitive to white males and quite capable of chewing them up as well—as million of downsized white male middle managers can attest to from bitter experience. Ranting about 'white male workplaces' ignores the realities of class, personality differences, and poor management practices. The dissatisfaction of diversity consultants may be aimed at white males in power, but the force of diversity reprogramming and accountability schemes fall on younger working and middle-class whites," writes Frederick R. Lynch. [18]

The results of diversity training programs have fallen far short of what has been promised to those organizational leaders buying in. From 1990 to 1994, there was a 34 percent increase in number of claims from 75,258 to 100,978 and a 38 percent increase in dollars from $130 million to $180 million awarded to individuals as a result of Equal Employment Opportunity Commission claims for sex, race, age discrimination, and sexual harassment. In addition, many millions of dollars in claims were settled outside the EEO and judicial systems. [19]

"A researcher close to the heart of the diversity machine let the cat out of the bag: People are afraid to find out that these programs don't work. There is a lot of money being made." [20]

SUMMARY

This analysis and evaluation of diversity training and its failures has provided us with solid groundwork with which to begin to work towards a solution to discrimination and harassment. Diversity training failed to meet its objectives because it focused on differences rather than on examining the skills needed to get the job done. It was believed that if differences were understood, they would disappear and that people would change, but they didn't. Instead the situation worsened and hostilities came out in the open. Backlash was inevitable.

Remedies were tried and failed because they were reactionary, and because they were most often based upon myths. Diversity training itself became a myth. The solution to the workplace dilemma lies in redirecting the focus and in choosing the right vehicle to effect the needed changes.

NOTES

1. "Managing Diversity in the Workplace," S. Kanu Kogod, *The 1992 Annual: Developing Human Resources*, p. 241.
2. "Diversity Study's Printing Error," *Wall Street Journal,* October 29, 1996.

3. "Diversity Training: Hope, Faith, and Cynicism," Allison Rossett and Terry Bickham, *Training,* January 1994, p. 41.

4. *Valuing Diversity,* Lennie Copeland and Lewis Griggs, 1987.

5. "From Affirmative Action to Affirming Diversity," *Harvard Business Review,* March/April 1990, pp. 107-117.

6. "Thanks, But No Thanks," Jack Gordon, *Training,* March 1996, p. 8.

7. "Corporate Experiences in Improving Women's Job Opportunities," *The Conference Board,* Report No. 755, 1979.

8. In 1996, the *American Society for Training and Development (ASTD)* published the first consolidated diversity training work entitled, "The Elements of Competence for Diversity Work," which draw on many current nationally-known authors.

9. "Training Can Damage Diversity Efforts," Sari Coudron, *Personnel Journal,* April 1993, p. 59.

10. Ibid.

11. "The Forgotten White Male," Glenn Rafkin, *Harvard Business Review,* July/August 1994.

12. "Where Diversity Training Goes Wrong," A.B. Karp and Nancy Sutton, *Training,* July 1993, p. 30.

13. "Backlash! The Challenge to Diversity Training," Michael Mobley and Tamara Payne, *Training and Development,* December 1992, p. 46.

14. Ibid.

15. "White Male Rage Sweeps America," *Washington Post,* February 9, 1995.

16. *The Diversity Machine: The Drive to Change the "White Male Workplace,"* Frederick R. Lynch, 1997.

17. The *Washington Post* article cited in "Backlash! The Challenge to Diversity Training," Michael Mobley and Tamara Payne, *Training and Development,* December 1992, p. 45.

18. *The Diversity Machine: The Drive to Change "White Male Workplace,"* Frederick R. Lynch, 1997, pp. 354-355.

19. Data taken from office of Program Operations from EEOC's Change Data Systems (CDS), *National Database,* 1994.

20. *The Diversity Machine: The Drive to Change the "White Male Workplace,"* Frederick R. Lynch, 1997, p. 196.

5

The Solution to the Workplace Dilemma

INTRODUCTION

Diversity training's focus on understanding and valuing human differences does not provide the solution to the workplace dilemma. Nor has it given us the workplace relationship skills necessary to work effectively with those who believe differently than we do. Dispensing information about how differences such as race, creed, or lifestyle might affect employees in the workplace without offering a set of skills to manage those differences is counterproductive at best.

We need not change our own values and belief systems in order to have good workplace relationships. We need only to develop the skills to manage our behavior toward all those who are different and not allow our personal likes, dislikes, biases, and prejudices to disrupt our ability to be productive. Bigotry, intolerance, discrimination and harassment behaviors seriously debilitate effectiveness, retention, and productivity—and therefore the company's bottom line.

As the workplace continues to diversify, employees of all races, creeds, and orientations will become the norm rather than the exception. To remain employable and meet the challenges ahead, it is essential that workers develop skill sets to interact effectively in today's diverse workplace. In order to develop the skills necessary to work effectively together, it is necessary to make a significant course correction.

COURSE CORRECTION

The solution to the workplace dilemma demands a strong definition of accepted human rights practices and supportive workplace relationship skills training. This includes:

1. A zero tolerance policy for discrimination and harassment practices;
2. Baseline workplace behavior standards expected of all employees; and
3. Supportive workplace relationship skills training program.

To put this course correction into operation you will need to:

- Gain the full commitment of all board members and senior management personnel to model, fully support, and enforce (1) a zero tolerance policy, (2) a set of workplace behavior standards, and (3) a supportive workplace relationships skills training program that makes it possible for employees to assess and move toward achieving a high level of proficiency in executing their relationship skills.
- Revisit all corporate documents: the vision, mission, values, goals, and action plans. Assure that a clear message is being sent to all employees and customers that your company will be free of all discrimination and harassment practices.
- Provide a set of behavior standards and a workforce relationship skills training program for all employees, that will be integrated into all company initiatives.
- Make employees accountable for their behaviors by building accountability practices through performance and development reviews; rewarding employees that model the company's zero tolerance discrimination and harassment policy and its workplace interaction standards; and incorporating accountability in promotion, transfer, discipline, and discharge assessments.
- Recruit, select, and hire to match your markets so that your company's demographics match your customer base. This visible population supports the premise that the company does not discriminate and assures that you get quality people who understand how to develop and respond to your markets.

Companies need to make it known that the cultures created within their workplaces are cultures to which all employees belong and where they all abide by similar human rights objectives. This message needs to be delivered not just by human resource personnel but by senior executives, line managers, as well as from one employee to another. With a zero tolerance policy in effect, employees will be put on alert that discrimination or harassment behaviors will not be tolerated. Employees will be expected to uphold this standard of behavior as part of all employer/employee/customer relationships.

A zero tolerance policy defines what is and what is not acceptable practice. It focuses on establishing standards of behavior. As the zero tolerance policy comes into effect, no discrimination or harassment behaviors will be tolerated from one employee toward another employee who either believes differently, whose culture is different, chooses a different lifestyle, has a different set of values, or is of a different sexual orientation.

The following steps are necessary to achieve the solution to the workplace dilemma:

1. Stop the Denial
2. Remove the Diversity Training Label
3. Focus on Behavior
4. Commit to a Plan of Action

Stop the Denial

It is hard to understand why, even in the face of hard evidence, company leaders continue to deny that discrimination and harassment exist. This is because harassment and discrimination are part and parcel of behavior patterns so ingrained within our social structure that they are frequently an acceptable part of company norms. The denial that these commonly accepted social behaviors are, indeed, malpractice results in a wide range of covert and overt behaviors. Inappropriate body language, verbal slurs, discounting, or devaluing, excluding, and negative labeling are all seen as part of social interaction. But when targeted toward a specific person or group of persons, they are, in fact, illegal. Denial of this can no longer be tolerated. That is what is meant by a zero tolerance policy.

Because discrimination and harassment practices are of a personal and sensitive nature, company leaders often sweep them under the rug rather than face the fact that these practices have been institutionalized as part of company norms. The many case studies we present in this book reveal the extent to which human rights malpractice still exists. Only the acceptance and adaptation of a zero tolerance policy can bring this denial to an end.

Denial of inappropriate and debilitating behavior plays itself out in many ways:

- Discrimination and harassment behavior patterns are embedded deeply and subtly into corporate cultures. They are a microcosm of society at large.
- In spite of high costs and growing evidence, elimination of discrimination and harassment practices is not a high priority in organizational budget allocations.
- Legal costs relating to discrimination and harassment are considered as administrative costs of doing business rather than the direct costs of sales or operations.
- Executives, managers, and supervisors often turn a deaf ear to these issues because they are unwilling to admit or are unaware that they are, in fact, active or passive participants.
- Many companies are wary and choose not to delve into areas related to personal values, prejudices, and biases. We found through our diversity training program experience that exposing volatile emotions without seeking resolution only antagonizes and increases the force of these destructive behaviors.
- Since there are no quick fixes and many businesses focus solely on the next quarter's earnings, and because this is an extremely complex problem for companies as well as for our society as a whole, it is much easier to ignore than fix discriminating and harassing behaviors.

Denial is costing companies millions of dollars. Destructive behavior patterns prevent companies from achieving their potential level of productivity and financial success. Oppressed, hurt, offended, and angry employees are not productive. Sick leave, employee turnover, and tardiness among stressed employees are only a few of the measurable losses. Immeasurable losses include those resulting from psychological damages, lower production, subtle sabotage, subterfuge, negative attitudes, and unsatisfactory service to customers.

Sensitive, emotionally explosive human rights issues are deeply embedded in the very fabric of American life. The negative mindset from which many of us harass and/or discriminate against another person or group is formed through our personal life experience. Only our strong commitment to a zero tolerance policy can expose, and therefore end, the denial of these disruptive behavior patterns.

Studies show that at least 85 percent of those people fired from their jobs are dismissed because of interpersonal limitations, a statistic that holds true at all organizational levels. It is their inability to get along with others—co-workers, bosses, subordinates or customers—that is the cause of their troubles, not poor technical skills. [1]

Diversity training programs that focus on our differences, rather than deal directly with the skills we need to address discrimination and harassment practices, support the denial. One Washington State-based human resource executive stated that in 1995 his company attempted to dismiss the problems of discrimination and harassment by offering administrators and most employees three or four hours of diversity awareness training in the hopes it would suffice. This is true all across the nation. Short-term training sessions were primarily focused on teaching about differences and historical inequities. Short-term training sessions did not seek resolution.

Many companies unwittingly bought programs that turned out to be ineffective and inappropriate. This type of shared angst, confrontation, name calling, and discounting the opinions of others did not help employees interact respectfully and trustingly with one another. These difficult sessions only served to promote divisiveness and dissension, and in the end gave diversity training its dubious reputation. To correct this demands a full turnaround: Stop the denial, face rampant practices of discrimination and harassment squarely, and begin with zero tolerance. Only then does the solution to the workplace dilemma becomes a possibility.

Remove the Diversity Label

Because diversity training elicits such sensitive and divisive reactions, we seriously question the value of using the term diversity in future workforce training programs. Many potential participants, in seeing training sessions with the diversity label, become resistant. Some refuse to attend; other refuse to participate fully while there. Diversity training programs have come to be seen as another example of gross cultural victimization.

The term diversity in the *Random House Webster's College Dictionary* is defined as the state or fact of being diverse, difference, unlikeness. In today's workplace, the term diversity connotes negative experience and a minority agenda to many employees. These sensitive issues with their subjective nature stir up our emotions. They require introspection and demand a change in behavior. Diversity training automatically raises internalized red flags and hinders a peacemaking, developmental process that moves toward the elimination of discrimination and harassment in our workplaces. [2]

Despite its buzzword status, there is no consensus in the business community on the meaning of the term diversity. Definitions of diversity range from narrow to very broad. Narrow definitions generally track federal equal employment opportunity law, which defines diversity in terms of race, gender, ethnicity, age, national origin, religion, and disability. Broader definitions encompass values, personality characteristics, education, and background characteristics such as geographic origin and economic status. Lifestyle is often added to diversity categories and covers a broad group of characteristics ranging from sexual orientation to formal and informal behavior styles. Family relationships necessitating flexible schedules or part-time work fall into this latter category. Most people accept the narrower definition of diversity. Some companies, however, are beginning to use the term *differences* rather than *diversity*.

Buzzwords come and go. Those that stay become part of meaningful and workable business terminology. Diversity has become a catchall term for so many human resource issues and has come to be associated with so many negative feelings that the diversity training label needs to be eliminated.

Once we stop the denial and remove the disruptive diversity labeling, we can commit to a plan of action based on a zero tolerance policy, workplace behavior standards, and workplace relationship skills training for all employees.

Focus on Behavior

Organizations require that employees bring their technical and functional skills to the workplace in order to fulfill the goals and objectives of the organization. It is appropriate, then, that organizations require employees to exhibit appropriate interpersonal behavior skills.

In order to effect reduction in discrimination and harassment, we must focus on the acceptable and unacceptable behavior practices in the workplace. Thus, diversity training's thrust to change employees' values and belief systems is the wrong focus.

Commit to a Plan of Action

A plan of action to eliminate discrimination and harassment practices within our workplaces includes the following steps:

1. Implement a top-down strategy;
2. Revisit and realign the organization's vision and mission statement; and

3. Integrate workplace relationship skills training into all business initiatives.

Implement a Top-Down Strategy

Leadership modeling from the board of directors and senior-level management staff is vital to bring about the cultural change necessary to eradicate discrimination and harassment. Without sincere commitment and follow-through from company leaders, those who practice discrimination and harassment will not take seriously the need to be accountable or recognize their behavior as harmful. A wake-up call from senior management to all employees who consciously or unconsciously mistreat fellow employees alerts everyone to the consequences meted out to those who disrupt productivity. Immediate and permanent elimination of destructive behaviors is expected. Written policy standards that define the acceptable and unacceptable behaviors expected of all employees increases awareness that full participation in workplace relationship development and training programs is expected from everyone. Management should post this written, zero tolerance policy in central locations and consistently refer to it in newsletters, e-mail, executive speeches, board meetings, and team sessions to keep everyone aware.

This cannot be viewed simply as a good thing to do. The bottom line depends on it. Millions and millions of dollars are paid out each year to lawyers and complainants. The litigation costs against U.S. companies for discrimination and harassment are astronomical. The productivity loss is even greater. None of us can afford to be part of that negative review, nor can we afford to contribute to our own or our company's demise.

Revisit and Realign Company Vision and Mission Statements

Company change managers need to: (1) Realign company vision and mission statements with a clear and direct zero tolerance policy that mandates healthy human rights practices; (2) Develop a set of interaction standards to demonstrate the level of interpersonal behavior expected of all employees. Establish dialogue across all lines of authority; (3) Position senior management as leadership models; (4) Ask for, and contract for, a buy-in from each individual; (5) Place vision and mission statements in highly visible locations; and (6) Alert employees and customers alike of the intent to maintain a discrimination and harassment free workplace. This takes awareness, education, visibility, and commitment.

Integrate the Development of Workplace Relationship Skills Training into All Business Initiatives

Most employers automatically assume that those applying for work have the necessary social skills with which to cope, but this is not always the case. Prospective employees are on their best behavior. Conscious or unconscious prejudices and biases are seldom revealed; nor are most interview sessions set up to expose them. Unconscious discrimination and harassment habit patterns learned from personal cultures and family systems remain hidden, consequently, what we see is not always what we get. It is important that workplace relationship skills training become an integral part of all business initiatives in order to support a holistic approach to human resource development. We cannot assume that all employees will have the necessary behaviors and skills to work effectively together, just as we cannot assume that all employees have what is called "common sense." By integrating workplace relationship skills training into all company initiatives, it will not be assumed that all employees are at the same skill level. By measuring all employees against workplace behavior standards expected from all, everyone stands equal. Millions of dollars in productivity, loss, and litigation could have been saved in the past and can be saved in the future by setting workplace behavior standards and integrating workplace relationship skills training programs with business initiatives and other workforce training programs.

SUMMARY

The solution to the workplace dilemma demands a zero tolerance policy for discrimination and harassment. Companies must develop workplace behavior standards of acceptable and unacceptable practices, with a supportive and integrated workplace relationship skills development and training program. This course correction is implemented through the following steps: Stop the denial; remove the diversity training label; focus on behavior; and commit to a plan of action. This action plan includes implementing a top down strategy, revisiting and revising the organization's vision and mission statements, and integrating workplace relationship skills training into all business initiatives.

NOTES

1. "Meeting Demands of Diversity Crucial for Workplace of the '90s," Gracie Bonds Staples, *Seattle Post-Intelligencer,* April 12, 1993.
2. "Where Diversity Training Goes Wrong," H.R. Karp and Nancy Sutton, *Training,* July 1993.

6

Workplace Relationship Skills
Development

INTRODUCTION

Discrimination and harassment are learned behaviors. They are formed from
the unconscious habit patterns made up of all life's experience and training.
These feelings are so much a part of us that we are not even aware of them.
However, since they are learned behaviors, they can be interrupted, changed,
and managed. Hostile interactions and destructive behaviors toward others in
ways that dominate, hurt, demean, overpower, undermine, diminish, or
discount for any reason constitute unacceptable workplace behavior. They do
not belong in the workplace—they must be confronted and changed.

A performance review, a supervisor's comment, or feedback from a fellow
employee might be all it takes to stimulate our awareness. Once aware of a
negative behavior, we can choose to change. That behavior can be intentionally
interrupted by developing high-quality workplace relationship skills. The ability to interact effectively with fellow employees and customers profoundly
affects our employability.

Whether we want to admit it or not, like everyone else, we bring a collection
of biases and prejudices into the workplace. Bias and prejudice are learned
from life experiences and from the persons who have made an impact upon our
lives, and therefore are emotionally embedded into the very fabric of our being.
With frequent repetition, bias and prejudice become ingrained as habits and are
experienced as part of everyday reality. They influence the perceptions of all
behavior. No one is exempt. They can fuel discrimination and harassment
practices and have the power to impede our ability to work effectively with
those that do not meet our own selective standards.

On the individual level, all relationships entertain the possibility of bias and
prejudice. In order to overcome this, workplace relationship skills are needed

to manage those biases and prejudices. Highly developed workplace relationship skills give us the ability to set bias and prejudice aside and work with others effectively, regardless of our differences.

On the group level, collective prejudice always expresses itself in some form of discrimination. Discrimination practices play a role in determining what neighborhoods people live in, what jobs they apply for, what schools they attend, how much money they make. Discrimination assigns value to skin color or gender and is the primary reason that people who are not a part of the dominant group have difficult and painful work experiences. Discrimination is exhibited in behavior, and in society, the patterned practices of these behaviors determine who gets what.

These detrimental behavior patterns are learned and, as such, can be unlearned and set aside. However, managing differences and remaining productive in today's volatile workplace takes highly developed workplace relationship skills. Skills to manage ourselves, continuous change, bias and prejudice, and workplace relationships are the ingredients of a workplace relationship skills program.

RELATIONSHIPS ARE ESSENTIAL

With the social atmosphere throughout the United States characterized by a high level of racial, sexual, and cultural tension, focusing on fair and respectful treatment for everyone is the strongest message institutions can give regarding their commitment to their workers. It is not in the employer's best interest to encourage the perception that co-workers or subordinates of another race or gender are *different* and therefore *lesser,* and certainly not that some groups are victims.

Getting along and listening to one another are reported as the two most important factors in work and team success. Effective interaction with fellow employees and mentoring one another along the way are key ingredients to promote individual success and for employers to develop productive employees.

Tom Peters, author of many best-selling business books, states, "Relationship is all there is." He believes that to survive in this global, technological and service economy, employees must be accountable for the quality of their workplace relationship skills. Even the most extraordinary breakthroughs in technology and the most ingenious application of the Internet will not save us from social breakdown if we do not have the skills necessary to work with one another—skills which we refer to as workplace relationship skills. [1]

Over one hundred senior managers were interviewed during our 1991 study, and almost all participants stated that to a large degree their success depended upon their ability to interact effectively with others. These executives reported that throughout their careers, it had been essential to continually work toward mastering successful workplace relationship skills. [2]

We agree with Stephen Covey, author of *The 7 Habits of Highly Effective People,* who states, "Communication is the most important skill in life. Good communication in the workplace transforms a collection of individuals into a strong, mutually supportive team. Communication builds the important ties that bind people together, inside the organization as well as outside." [3]

THE MODEL

The solution to the workplace dilemma consists of three steps: (1) Implement and enforce a zero tolerance policy for discrimination and harassment behavior practices in the workplace; (2) Develop and publish a set of workplace behavior standards of acceptable and unacceptable behavior in the workplace; and (3) Provide a workplace relationship skills training program for all employees.

Rather than asking employees to change their values and belief systems (their prejudices and biases), as is done in diversity training courses, this model focuses on a definition of acceptable and unacceptable workplace behaviors and a zero tolerance process that requires that all employees be accountable for their behavior. To meet these workplace policies and behavior standards, the organization must offer a relationship skills training program that teaches employees the skills to work together effectively regardless of their differences. Meaningful involvement with others, adjusting quickly to change, and continuous learning about self and others are a few of the many qualities expected of employees with a high level of relationship skills. (See Table A: Workplace Relationship Skills Continuum.)

Three unique programs are the core of our model: (1) Managing our Mind-Talk,™ (2) Understanding Organizational MindTalk,™ and (3) A Workplace Relationship Skills ToolKit.™

MANAGING OUR MindTalk™

The effectiveness of all our relationships depends upon the quality of our MindTalk,™ which consists of the conversations that take place inside ourselves, to ourselves, about ourselves and others. MindTalk™ says things like:

"Why can't she learn to speak English?"
"I'm too fat."
"Dad would be proud of me now."
"I wish he would just go away and I wouldn't have to deal with this."
"Yes! It's good for me."
"I need and deserve this promotion."

MindTalk™ determines our acceptance of ourselves and others, our values and beliefs, our stereotypes and biases, our emotional and physical health, our self-esteem and our self-image, our successes and failures. The conversations that each of us has inside our minds determine our ability to conquer fear and cope with stress. Managing our MindTalk™ is our most important life work. In the end, MindTalk™ is what and who we are and controls all of our behavior.

Internal Operating Committee (IOC)

The easiest way to understand MindTalk™ is to think of it as a committee working inside the mind, a set of internal figures that function more or less as advisors. Collectively, they form an advisory group, or Internal Operating Committee (IOC). This committee assists us in organizing, planning, designing, implementing, and controlling our life's experience. This committee meets metaphorically around an internal conference table to discuss our interests, our needs, and our stresses. With their help, we determine what we believe, how we manage life, and how we interact with others.

These committee members are formed from trace images of each of our childhood models and lifetime mentors. In fact, anyone who has influenced our lives to some degree may end up sitting in on this committee. These voices form the source material that feeds our MindTalk™; these are the voices we listen to. In time they become stereotyped according to the roles they play, such as Caretaker, Critic, Boss, or Spiritual Advisor. (See Table B: Internal Operating Committee [IOC] Members.)

In any given situation, any one of the members might attempt to assume leadership. For example, if the internal Boss assumes leadership, we might hear such comments as: "It better be right." "Don't make a mistake!" "Get it in on time!" On the other hand, if our Caretaker takes over, we would hear comments like: "I need to take more time to relax and enjoy my friends." "I know I am going to be all right." "I'll take a walk after lunch."

We often get opposing messages from the conflicting agendas of internal figures who fight to control our IOC. For instance, discrimination and harassment behaviors usually develop from interactions led by the Abuser, the Critic, the Doubter, or the Dictator. Conversely, Caretaker, Mother, and Friend figures would likely fight to protect me from discrimination and harassment behaviors.

The IOC often has members who are in conflict with other members, paralleling roles our life models and/or mentors played. They also may have agendas that are in conflict with members of another person's committee. When one set of internal figures is in conflict with another set, the two often vie for top position. Typical of conflicts that can arise in both personal and professional settings would be Boss vs. Rebel; Dictator vs. Child; Employee vs. Mother; or Female vs. Abuser. (See Table C: Typical Conflicting Figures.)

Those who experience the most success in relationships are those whose internal figures are comfortable in allowing the leadership of their IOC to move freely from one figure to another and thus respond to the situation at hand rather than expecting or demanding repeat performances of past encounters or predetermined results. Individuals who have difficulty in establishing effective relationships with themselves and others are those whose internal figures fight to retain rigid control. For instance, a person whose Dictator prevails—with its emotional inflexibility, need to control, and always be right as the Leader—has a difficult time learning how to accept differences in other people and is, in fact, not responding to the situation at hand. This prevents him or her from seeing the situation with a clear vision and utilizing those professional relationship skills necessary to address the current problem. Managed Mind-Talk™ lets us put the Dictator to rest and focus on current problems with clarity and impunity.

Companion Emotional Reactions

Emotional reactions impact body chemistry and physical and emotional health, and thus affect all of our personal and workplace relationships. MindTalk™ has companion emotional reactions to all mind and body experiences. With each remembered experience, MindTalk™ recalls a landscape of emotions. Through MindTalk™ we have the ability to scare or soothe ourselves. Through using our MindTalk,™ we have the ability to effectively handle the situation at hand, or allow ourselves to be victimized by it.

The Outside Observer

The unique ability to view ourselves from the outside and observe our own thoughts, feelings, and behavior is what makes us human. This ability to look at ourselves inside ourselves plays a critical role in managing our Internal Operating Committee. We have the ability to act as an outside observer to our IOC's discussions and yet remain critically involved. As the outside observer, we might say to our IOC something like, "I can see the part I played in this conflict." "I can hear the negative comments I am saying to myself about how fat I am." Or, "There is that old habit, I always lash out and use that tone of voice when I feel threatened."

The IOC should function *only* as an advisory group. Danger lurks when it controls rather than advises. In the end, we must manage our committee and not let our committee manage us. We must recognize and accept responsibility for the choices we each make and the way we manage the behavior that results from our MindTalk.™

PERCEPTIONS

The primary function of the IOC lies in the management of perceptions. Perceptions are essentially a collage, or composite, of mental snapshots taken from all we see, hear, taste, smell, touch, feel, and experience. Perceptions form our view of reality and influence everything we do. Perceptions enter our mind through our senses and are stored in our mind as thoughts and feelings. They provide us with a frame of reference about our life. They are the lens through which we view the world.

Perceptions Are Stored Inside The Mind In Clusters

Perceptions are stored in the mind in clusters grouped together by similar subject matters such as family, community, business, organizations, religion, politics, race, sexuality, gender, relationships, or communications. When we are asked about any given subject, a group of related perceptions emerges from those thoughts and feelings to help form our opinion about it. Notice that when we hear such names as O.J. Simpson, Rodney King, Anita Hill, or President Clinton we come up with a certain set or cluster of perceptions. In contrast, the mention of our mother, our best friend, or perhaps a fondly remembered teacher brings about feelings that color opinions in an entirely different way. These are perceptions; these are personal views of these particular people.

Perceptions That Are Repeated Frequently Become Habit Patterns

From perceptions (thoughts and feelings), we create the automatic responses that become habit patterns. Habit patterns, formed at the unconscious level, control behavior. Examples of habit patterns range from everyday acts such as tying our shoes, brushing our teeth, or starting our car to emotional and psychological reactions that form beliefs or value systems and eventually create bias. Once a cluster of perceptions takes hold and becomes ingrained as habit, it affects the work of each member of the Internal Operating Committee. Habitual behavior is often overlooked by our IOC. Perceptions set direction, control behavior, and affect all our relationships.

Filtering Systems

Perceptions form filtering systems through which we screen everything we think, feel, and see. Filters screen reality, control interaction processes and eventually govern how we listen, act, and react. The density or fluidity of these filters, and whether they remain open or are closed to new perceptions, impacts all relationships. When we are threatened or unsure of ourselves, our filters become more dense. When we are relaxed and in a safe environment, our filters expand and open up to new perceptions. The secret to being relaxed and having open filters in any given situation lies in managing our MindTalk.™ Well-managed MindTalk™ is the secret to achieving high-level workplace rela-tionship skills.

HOW TO MANAGE MindTalk™ AND PERCEPTIONS

Through MindTalk™ we manage our personal and workplace growth, relationships, life experiences, and behaviors. Managing MindTalk™ involves questioning perceptions, challenging clusters of perceptions, interrupting habit patterns, and controlling filters.

Questioning Perceptions

To be an effective participant in work and life, we need to question the perceptions we have about ourselves and the way we relate to those who are different from us, such as male or female, black or white, old or young, heterosexual or homosexual.

Challenging Clusters Of Perceptions

Group memberships—including those involving church, nationality, race, or politics—tend to demand particular behaviors that identify members with each other and therefore bond them to the group. We must guard against having our individuality sacrificed by any group. Continually adapting our behavior to others keeps perceptions confined. Furthermore, in order to retain these adapted behaviors, our perceptions must be kept narrowed, thus understanding and acceptance of others is limited. Narrow vision limits personal and workplace effectiveness, because it prevents understanding and acceptance.

Interrupting Habit Patterns

We learn discriminative behavior patterns from those who have raised us. Self-limiting behavior patterns become so ingrained that they define reality. When fully accepted, their adaptation to a variety of situations becomes automatic. In order to interrupt their flow, we must first become aware of them and how limiting and destructive they can become. Understanding that, we can make a conscious choice as to how we want to respond; we can choose to keep them or choose to change them.

Controlling Filters

Filters become dense or fluid in direct relation to how the situation is perceived. Whether or not filters are dense or fluid is also a habit pattern. However, when we experience certain types of conditions, we tend to go unconscious, go on automatic, return to historic habit patterns, stop listening, or relate inappropriately. Trauma, stress, anger, depression, hunger, pain, fatigue, body chemical change, or threat are examples of these conditions. Each of these situations is perceived by our bodies as life-threatening; consequently, our most natural response at these times is to protect ourselves and keep our filters closed. (See Table D: Examples of Closed-Filter Situations.)

The labeling of homosexual behavior as immoral, sinful, or bestial by certain conservative religious groups is an example of closed filters. To label others in this way, requires that they must first be devalued as human beings. This demonsrates how closed filters operate on a social level.

However, when we are in a situation where we feel safe, trusted, loved, listened to, free, respected or appreciated, or when the situation is nonjudgmental or open, filters tend to become more fluid. Free to be aware in the moment, we open ourselves to new and different perceptions and relationships. In these instances, filters are open to suggestion and change. (See Table E: Examples of Open-Filter Situations.)

Just as behavior is learned and can therefore be changed and managed, so can the filters that control behavior be changed. Controlling our filters is important in managing ourselves.

ORGANIZATIONAL MindTalk™

Our Individual MindTalk™ not only influences our personal behavior, but it influences, and is influenced, by Organizational MindTalk.™ Organizational MindTalk™ is what the organization says inside itself about itself and others, which identifies its culture and is the basis for all of its behavior.

We chose a similar metaphor to describe Organizational MindTalk™ as we used in describing Individual MindTalk.™ The Organization's Internal Operating Committee (IOC) is composed of individuals who bring specific skill sets to the workplace to fulfill the organization's goals. Organizational units expect their employees to bring to the workplace a set of skills to satisfy the specific functions of the unit and to meet the objectives of the organization. Examples are sets of skills that fulfill the functions in sales, marketing, human resources, product development, finance, leadership, administration, management, etc.

This means individuals should bring only their IOC members with the appropriate skill sets to the workplace. In practice, however, employees bring both their skill set members and their personal IOC members to the workplace.

The integration of the organizational leadership's mandates and the employees' IOCs create the organizational culture.

The culture is then described through written and unwritten policies and procedures, which establish the acceptable and unacceptable behavior practices for the organization and each of its units.

The culture of each organizational unit will be unique because of the different functions, skill sets, and personal IOCs of members. For example, in a sales unit, the major business function is to promote and sell the company's products and services. The employee must have the skills and experiences necessary to support the sales function, such as presentation skills, product knowledge, and relationship skills. Sales employees will bring their specific sales skills and their personal IOC members, that form the subculture for the sales department. This subculture defines the written and unwritten policies, which establishes the acceptable and unacceptable behaviors of their sales unit. The sales staff may have behaviors which are perfectly acceptable in their subculture, but are unacceptable when presented to employees in the product delivery unit, or any other unit, or to external customers.

Organizational teams follow a similar internal process. Members are expected to bring specific skill sets to meet the team objectives. Teams are less formal; therefore, the organization's functions and the application of the employee skill sets are less rigidly enforced, depending on the team's current objective. This process provides an environment that allows employees to bring a wider range of their IOC members to the team. The team establishes their subculture with its acceptable and unacceptable behavior practices.

The organizational culture and subcultures of the units and teams set in place the behavior practices of the organization; therefore, to eliminate discrimination and harassment in organizations, it is essential to establish a standard of behavior practices for the organization and all of its units and teams.

Each individual is ultimately responsible for his or her workplace behaviors; however, in implementing the action plan for our workplace solution, it is essential to realize the powerful impact of the organization's culture and subcultures on individual behavior practices.

SUMMARY

Workplace relationship skills development is based on an understanding of individual and organizational MindTalk™ and the application of management principles to effect behavior changes in the workplace. By developing an understanding of the significant role MindTalk™ plays in all behaviors, actions, and reactions, we can understand its importance in establishing and maintaining effective relationships. Managing MindTalk™ is as easy as remembering to: (1) Question our perceptions; (2) Challenge our clusters of perceptions; (3) Interrupt our habit patterns; and (4) Control our filters. The MindTalk™ Management Process, the core of the Workplace Relationship Skills ToolKit,™ offers employees significant tools to increase their workplace relationship skills.

NOTES

1. *Liberation Management: Necessary Disorganization for the Nanosecond Nineties,* Tom Peters, 1992.

2. Revised from a 1991 study for the book, *The Rise of the Corporate Superstars,* Hellen Hemphill, Ph.D.

3. *The 7 Habits of Highly Effective People: Powerful Lessons in Personal Change,* Stephen R. Covey, 1989, p. 239.

7

Workplace Relationship Skills ToolKit™

INTRODUCTION

By using newfound MindTalk™ skills, new channels of thinking, feeling, and behaving will be opened. By applying MindTalk™ process skills to each component of the Workplace Relationship Skills ToolKit™ you can become your own coach, mentor, supervisor, teacher, or therapist. The ToolKit™ contains model designs or sets of questions that can be responded to individually and or in groups. They are designed to be scanned through, taken one by one, or responded to individually, as units, or collectively as the need arises. How the ToolKit™ is used is a matter of individual choice, as is every other choice you make concerning behavior. Using the ToolKit™ will support the management of bias and prejudice, improve the ability to interact with fellow employees and customers, increase personal and professional effectiveness, and increase productivity in the workplace.

The following four MindTalk™ Management skills are incorporated in each of the components of the ToolKit™:

1. Question Perceptions;
2. Challenge Clusters of Perceptions;
3. Interrupt Habit Patterns; and
4. Control Filters.

The components of the Workplace Relationship Skills ToolKit™ are:

- Increase Listening Skills;
- Interrupt And Reframe Negative MindTalk™;
- Interrupt And Control Negative Emotional Habit Patterns;
- Interrupt The Victimization Cycle;
- Understand The Communication Process;

- Improve Conflict Management Skills; and
- Explode Relationship Myths.

(See Table F: Workplace Skills Relationship ToolKit,™ whose contents reiterate this overview.)

INCREASE LISTENING SKILLS

"Listening to understand" means looking at an issue from the other person's point of view, however different from ours it may be. Effective relationship management depends upon those listening skills. Listening to understand develops the ability to resolve even the most difficult workplace problems. If we are intent on furthering our own point of view, however, we are filtering out the other's message, and not listening. But if we are willing to give our full attention to others, we can relate effectively with people who think and believe differently than we do. Neither side may choose to change, but both parties need to be heard. The advantage in beginning discussions this way is that both parties retain their dignity and self-worth.

Each of us has learned to value certain ideas, customs, or ideologies more than others. By listening effectively, we increase awareness of those different values. Opening filters creates the potential to alter perceptions and creates the possibility of incorporating new ideas into the present reality. Whether we do that or not is purely up to us. Listening does not demand change, it only demands that we pay attention.

"To listen is to pay attention, take an interest, care about, take to heart, validate, acknowledge, to be moved by . . . appreciate. Listening is in fact so central to human existence as to often escape notice; or, rather, it appears in so many guises that it is seldom grasped as the overarching need that it is," states Michael Nichols in his premier book *The Lost Art of Listening*. He goes on to say that, "our lives are co-authored in dialogue. . . . We define and sustain ourselves in conversations with others," and describes the key role that listening plays in effective relationship management. [1]

In *The 7 Habits of Highly Effective People*, Stephen Covey emphasizes the essential nature of empathic listening skills to enhance work and social relationships. He describes empathic listening as "listening with the intent to understand. It means seeking first to really understand. Empathic listening gets inside another person's frame of reference. You look out through it, you see the world the way they see the world, you understand their paradigm, you understand how they feel. Empathy is not sympathy. You listen with your ears, your eyes, and your heart. You listen for feeling, for meaning. You listen for behavior. You sense, you intuit, you feel. Empathic listening is so powerful because it gives you accurate data to work with. Instead of projecting your own thoughts, feelings, motives, and interpretations, you are dealing with the reality inside another person's heart and head. You are focused on receiving the deep communication of another human soul." [2]

According to a recent national job analysis study, listening and responding to customer concerns is one of the primary activities in today's workplace. We all admire a good listener. Because of that, honing our listening skills gives us considerable advantage in the workplace. Being a good listener is not a natural attribute, but there is no mystique to it. It is a learned behavior. (See Table G: Increase Listening Skills.)

INTERRUPT AND REFRAME NEGATIVE MindTalk™

MindTalk™ controls our life! The source of MindTalk,™ the Internal Operating Committee (IOC) plans, designs, organizes, and implements behavior and affects all relationships. What each of us tells ourselves about ourselves and others has the power to send our self-esteem skyrocketing to the top or plummeting to the bottom.

Words we use in MindTalk™ have a strong impact on our quality of life and the quality of our relationships. Some words have a painful impact. They hurt others and cripple us. By managing negative MindTalk™ and revamping our vocabulary, we can change our lives. (See Table H: Pain-to-Power Vocabulary Chart.)

The major source of fear for most people revolves around relationships, and, for many, negative MindTalk™ revolves around limitations in managing interactions with others. MindTalk™ that focuses on past failures and/or fear of failure in the future often sets up a continuum of negative thoughts and feelings. The same painful messages are repeated again and again, the same unconstructive internal arguments, the same lack of focus on effective actions, plans, and solutions. Yet over 90 percent of what we tell ourselves to worry about never happens. [3] Unfortunately, it is this useless worry over things that never did, and most likely never will, happen that makes us sick. Freeing ourselves from this habitual negative MindTalk™ renews our sense of well-being by giving us the physical and emotional strength to handle problems more realistically. (See Table I: Interrupt and Reframe Negative MindTalk.™) Changing negative MindTalk™ is much like trying to change the way we tie our shoes. Doing something differently feels awkward at first, but with practice it becomes automatic.

INTERRUPT AND CONTROL NEGATIVE EMOTIONAL HABIT PATTERNS

By themselves, feelings are neither good nor bad. But they are clues to our most crucial concerns, our deepest commitments, our needs, and our wants. Gathered from total life experience, they form the data upon which we base our emotional reactions. In short, we have learned to feel the way we do. We have learned how to express feelings in the manner that we do. By interrupting the flow of our habitual negative emotional patterns, we learn to express feelings in new ways—ways that do not hurt ourselves or others.

When perceptions that create automatic negative reactions such as alienation, anxiety, apathy, hostility, and anger are cleared away, we increase the opportunity to become more open in our relationships with others. This process includes the ability to calm, compose, and soothe ourselves. Calming ourselves gives us opportunity to shake off any rampant irritability, impatience, frustration, or anxiety that we might carry into our relationships.

Handling feelings intelligently so they are appropriate is a mastery level skill. In *Emotional IQ*, Daniel Goleman describes the following ways that people are emotionally intelligent: (1) Know one's emotions; (2) Manage emotions; (3) Motivate oneself; (4) Recognize emotions in others; and (5) Handle relationships. [4]

The better we understand emotional intelligence and its resulting emotional habit patterns, the more effective we will be in handling our feelings and our relationships. According to author Howard Gardner, the key to self-knowledge is, "access to one's own feelings and the ability to discriminate among them and draw upon them to guide behavior." [5] This ability to access and understand feelings will provide insight into our personal relationships and our interactions with others at work. More than that, it will help us understand ourselves and why we do the things we do.

The emotional content of our interactions is the glue that holds good relationships together. However, in personal and professional environments, over 50 percent of all we say to one another consists of an informational exchange with little or no emotional content. Most often we are told to check our feelings at the door. This exclusion of feelings fosters distancing and limits the development of healthy work relationships. This is the opposite of what is needed for success in today's service-oriented workplace, where feelings form the basis of good employer-employee-customer relations.

Emotional learning that occurs early in life and fosters behavior patterns that are essentially destructive, is hard to eradicate entirely, even in people who as adults feel that their behavior is inappropriate. "The emotions of prejudice are formed in childhood, while the beliefs that are used to justify them come later on," explains Thomas Pettigrew, a social psychologist at the University of California at Santa Cruz. "Later in life you want to change your prejudice, but it is far easier to change your intellectual beliefs than your deep feelings. For instance, many Southerners confess that even though in their minds they no longer feel prejudice against blacks, they feel squeamish when they shake hands with a black person. These feelings are left over from what they learned in their families as children." [6]

Children learn most of their communication skills in the home; therefore, kids who are chronic targets of insults and criticism grow into adults who tend to resort to the same negative language. Whatever is learned as a child is viewed by that child as normal and, if endorsed or encouraged, becomes ingrained as lifelong habit patterns and standards of behavior. Understanding that, although ingrained, habit patterns can be changed.

Because many feelings are based on unconscious habit patterns, most people remain unaware of what they are feeling. Unconscious negative emotional habit patterns control our behavior and destroy our relationships. They are dangerous and self-destructive. They cause us to be involved in discrimination and harassment practices. We can't afford them. (See Table J: Interrupt and Control Negative Emotional Habit Patterns.)

The bottom line is to know that we can choose to interrupt our habitual negative emotional patterns, and we can refuse to allow them to rule or ruin our relationships. Feelings, like thoughts, are part of being human. But feelings are just feelings. They come and they go. The goodly portion of the negative feelings that we experience in any situation are most often products of past perceptions. It is possible to feel anger or frustration yet choose not to act on it. Choosing to express feelings more appropriately and in ways that do not abuse or manipulate others, allows us to manage our lives. It begins and ends with MindTalk.™

INTERRUPT THE VICTIMIZATION CYCLE

We learn how to become victims from childhood. This negative habit pattern carries into adulthood. Once viewed and understood as the negative habit pattern it is, it can be interrupted.

We all have choices. In fact, just knowing that being victimized is learned behavior frees most people. Not giving away our personal power to the control or subjugation of another frees us from playing the role of victim. Since victim behavior is learned, it can be changed. Internal pain from past perceptions draws our attention inward, and we become self-absorbed. Not understanding the role we play in this process, most of us fall into believing that we are being victimized by sources outside of ourselves. As we mature we come to realize the roles we play in victimizing ourselves. Part of being adult is accepting responsibility for our behavior and allowing others to do the same. It is possible to learn to identify and relax the parts of ourselves that interfere with choice, thus releasing these constraints. Perceptions such as criticism, fear, and hurt that create automatic emotional reactions and perpetuate the victimization cycle can be cleared away.

The victim continuously plays one of the key roles in what family therapy systems refer to as the Persecutor-Victim-Rescuer Emotional Triangle. The internal figures who relate to these roles take turns running the Internal Operating Committee. This triangle of behaviors is played out in the majority of re-lationship settings.

Descriptions of these three key roles are:

- *Persecutor:* The oppressor. The abuser who is judgmental, highly critical, who uses fear to control.
- *Victim:* The sufferer. The one who withdraws emotionally. The martyr.
- *Rescuer:* The comforter and protector of the victim. The excuse-maker for the persecutor.

When we respond as either persecutor, victim, or rescuer, we give away our personal power by playing into someone else's needs. This causes difficulties in work relationships as well as in personal relationships. In any of these three roles, habitual negative emotional reactions and negative MindTalk™ fuel the victimization cycle. Feelings of helplessness set the stage. These feelings can be changed with positive MindTalk.™

Whenever negative emotions such as anger or jealousy surface, they can be interrupted and robbed of their power by realizing how abdicating the responsibility for our own reactions causes us to fall prey to someone else's negative emotional reactions. By giving away our power, we end up powerless. If we do not give away our power, we cannot become victimized. When we are victimized, we are the one who made the choice to give away that power. Not being victimized begins by making the conscious choice not to give away personal power. (See Table K: Interrupt the Victimization Cycle.)

UNDERSTAND THE COMMUNICATION PROCESS

Organizations expect their employees to arrive at the workplace with effective communication skills. There is the expectation that these skills were learned early in life and are a natural part of a healthy person's repertoire. Anyone who has spent much time in an organizational setting knows this is a myth. The fact is that over 85 percent of all the terminations that take place in U.S. businesses are due to relationship problems. Most of these problems stem from the inability of people to communicate effectively. Ineffective communication results in poor coordinating efforts and lower productivity. Undercurrents of tension, gossip, and rumor lead to increased turnover and absenteeism. [7]

Learning how to communicate well is a complex process and involves many different components all operating at the same time. The exchange of infor-mation is both verbal and nonverbal, involves both the conscious and unconscious, and is filtered through our perceptions as it is being sent or received. Further complicating this process is the fact that each situation demands a different behavior. We behave, and therefore communicate, dif-ferently in a formal dinner setting than in a team problem-solving session.

Each social situation engenders a different energy level that can range from being depressive to high-spirited. Emotionally centering this process is necessary to create a climate of trust so that both parties will want to continue listening to one another.

Preparing to send a message to another person begins through an unconscious process. We tend to sort through and assess our perceptions about the situation, then plan and design our message. If it is quite important to us, we may review it first. We may even rehearse it.

Behind every communication there is hidden MindTalk™ and the nuances resulting from it. All perceptions are filtered through MindTalk™ by all parties involved. Each of us presents to and listens to the interaction from our own frame of reference.

In fact, what we actually say carries the least amount of weight with our listeners. Our verbal message only makes up a small percentage of the impact. Our voice tone and its intensity accounts for approximately one-third of what holds another's attention and our nonverbal message or body language commands over one-half of the impact that we have on others in all of our communications. [8]

Some things to keep in mind when learning how to communicate more effectively are: (1) Do not place blame on the other person; they will stop listening; (2) Do not discount; keep comments in the present; and (3) Own the part each party plays in the interaction by using the pronoun "I" instead of "you" or "we."

To be more effective when receiving messages, remember that all messages contain both content and emotions. To be a good listener, concentrate on the speaker, open filters, and listen for both facts and feelings. Try to understand, not judge, the message that is being sent. This means simply paying attention to listening. That is, learn to listen to the whole message before internally formulating a response.

To verify that the message was received in the way that the sender intended it, ask for feedback, question the sender to verify content, paraphrase the content, listen for nonverbal cues, and take careful note of any underlying feelings and expressions.

Poor listening skills result in ineffective interactions that create serious problems. These include: A sense of being misunderstood, isolated, lonely or powerless; feelings of alienation, anger and hostility; the loss of self esteem; and acts of discrimination, harassment, bias, and stereotyping.

Attentive listening brings about effective interactions that have very different outcomes. People feel understood, heard, included, accepted, honored, respected, important, cared about, trusted. This alone could increase productivity and work effectiveness. Effective communication is the key to a workplace in which people feel good about themselves and others around them.

IMPROVE CONFLICT MANAGEMENT SKILLS

Conflicts arise from the clash of perceptions, goals, and values in areas where people have vested interest. They happen in almost any area where human beings work together. Being able to negotiate and resolve conflict is a primary skill in effectively managing our workplace relationships.

We learned how to manage discord and resolve conflict from our parents and other significant people as we grew up. To complicate matters, we learned different processes. And while conflict can be resolved through almost any type of process, not all of these processes are adaptable to the workplace culture. Withdrawal or aggression may be acceptable in certain circumstances, but they prove counterproductive in the workplace. To resolve conflict in the workplace, new ground rules need to be formatted regarding what is and what is not acceptable behavior. These ground rules formulate and maintain the company culture.

In conflict situations, participants become sensitive. Emotional behaviors may escalate rather than resolve conflict. These behaviors may be unconscious, but as we have learned, they can become conscious, interrupted and changed. (See Table L: Improve Conflict Management Skills: Behaviors That Escalate Conflict.)

Instead, when working toward resolution, all parties concerned should discover as many areas of agreement as possible and build on that common ground to resolve conflict. Rules for managing conflict need to be established. Included in those basic rules should be who will do what, where, and when. (See Table M: Improve Conflict Management Skills: Behaviors That Resolve Conflict.)

EXPLODE RELATIONSHIP MYTHS

To understand ourselves, our relationships, and our company better, try examining clusters of perceptions in light of common but deceptive relationship myths. Relationship myths are common beliefs that most of the time have no basis in truth and only continue because they are never questioned. (See Table N: Explode Relationship Myths.)

But we can question them, and we can change them. All it takes is constructive MindTalk.™ To use our MindTalk™ to the best advantage, always remember to:

1. *Question Perceptions*: Question our perceptions while listening carefully to all sides of the arguments as the negotiation process expands those perceptions. Understand that everyone has a unique frame of reference that you can learn from.
2. *Challenge Clusters Of Perceptions*: Realize that individual clusters of perceptions present only a part of the picture. There is always more to know about the subject area that is being discussed.

3. *Interrupt Emotional Habit Patterns*: You can choose to interrupt emotional habit patterns by being consciously aware of emotional reactions. You don't always have to act on your feelings.

4. *Control Filters*: Conflict resolution is often seen as a stressful process, so remember that when under stress, filters become more dense and closed off to the outside input necessary to negotiate a successful resolution. Remain consciously aware that when your filters are closing, you are making that decision.

SUMMARY

The Workplace Relationship Skills ToolKit™ provides employees with a series of processes to develop their workplace behavior skills, increase their effectiveness, and enhance their workplace environment. Managing our Mind-Talk™ is at the core of developing high level workplace relationship skills. The Workplace Relationship Skills ToolKit,™ with its individual and group training techniques and exercises, is valuable as a team-building process and/or incorporated into the organization's human development program.

NOTES

1. *The Lost Art of Listening,* Michael P. Nichols, 1995, p.13.

2. *The 7 Habits of Highly Effective People: Powerful Lessons in Personal Change,* Stephen R. Covey, 1989, p. 238.

3. *Who's Driving Your Bus? Codependent Business Behaviors of Workaholics, Perfectionists, Martyrs, Tap Dancers, Caretakers, and People-Pleasers,* Ernie Larsen and Jeannette Goldstein, 1993, p. 18.

4. *Emotional Intelligence: Why It Can Matter More than IQ,* Daniel Goleman, 1995, p.37.

5. Ibid.

6. "White Men and Managing Diversity," Duncan Spelman, *The Diversity Factor,* Spring 1993, p. 14.

7. "Meeting Demands of Diversity Crucial for Workplace of the '90s," Gracie Bonds Staples, *Seattle Post-Intelligencer,* April 12, 1993.

8. *Communicating at Work,* Tony Allesandra, Ph.D., and Phil Hunsaker, Ph.D., 1993.

8

Implementation

INTRODUCTION

To decrease and eliminate discrimination and harassment practices, companies need to have both their principles and their practices understood and applied at all levels in the organization. Principles are the foundation on which applications and practices are built. They are the primary truths or distinctive opinions that form the basis of company culture. They tell *why* we should do certain things, whereas practices tell more specifically *what* to do, that is, how to carry out these principles.

Unless employees understand the principles, or the *why* of any particular task, they will become bewildered when the situation changes and requires different procedures. Explaining *what* but not *why* creates task-oriented employees dependent upon company rules. This renders them incapable of independent thinking or personal growth and without the adaptability necessary to survive in today's work world. When we teach practices without teaching principles, we make employees dependent on the company for further instruction and direction. In the end, this robs both the company and the employee of satisfaction and productivity.

Successful leaders build company principles into the center of their lives, their agreements, and their contracts. Employers and employees feel part of the common endeavor; bonding takes place in the process of striving to achieve common goals. This is apparent in the company's management process and mission statement and in interaction and relationships with others.

The guiding principle apparent in a strong company leader is the desire to build a productive and profitable workforce. The benefits reaped from this type of management approach are employees who are effective and yet remain free to develop their own potential. Practices that would be an outgrowth of such guiding principles would be to:

- Establish clear and vigorously enforced policies against discrimination and sexual harassment and set up grievance procedures.
- Establish acceptable basic workplace behavior standards.
- Establish how criticism will be constructively presented.
- Ensure barrier-free access to all work information and facilities.
- Prohibit corporate-sponsored or sanctioned memberships that discriminate on the basis of gender, race, or ethnicity.
- Negotiate constructive functional alliances with employees.
- Offer continual training to upgrade employees' technical and interpersonal skills.

EMPLOYER LIABILITY

Employers are not liable for the beliefs of their employees. But employers are responsible for the illegal behavior and conduct of their employees, and are therefore liable according to law. Employees who break rules nullify company policy, make void their company's culture and norms, and put their company at risk.

Liability for discrimination arises not because of individual employee beliefs or attitudes, but as a result of an employee's illegal conduct. For example, in 1994 San Diego Gas & Electric Co. was ordered to pay $3 million to a black former employee. Among numerous instances of illegal conduct, the court found that the employee had been called "nigger," "coon," and "boy." In the presence of a manager, a co-worker had threatened to "beat (his) black ass." Racial and sexual graffiti about him had been written in the men's room. No one had been disciplined for these activities. [1]

In a recent sex discrimination case, a Wal-Mart employee who had been sexually harassed was initially awarded $50 million (reduced to $5 million on appeal). A female stockroom worker was subjected to frequent comments about her anatomy by her supervisor. He also attempted to kiss her. When she complained to the store manager, the manager did nothing to stop the harassment. Wal-Mart attempted unsuccessfully to defend itself by showing that it had a strong policy against sexual harassment and that the company did not condone such behavior. The company did not discipline its employee because no mechanism was in place to do so. [2] This is why an enforcement policy for zero tolerance is essential. The zero tolerance policy establishes as fact that the company has a system in place and that infraction of it is illegal and punishable.

Companies, intending to protect themselves from the cost of litigation, have opened the door for a lucrative new industry—discrimination insurance. The Lexington Insurance Company, based in Boston, Massachusetts, began selling policies for litigation protection in 1992. A spokesperson for Lexington stated that the company has 450 clients with active policies in 1997, nearly 30 percent more than in 1996. They expect to have similar growth during next year. [3] The added expense for insurance would be unnecessary if employers enforced a zero tolerance policy for discrimination and harassment in their workplaces, established acceptable and unacceptable behavior standards, and provided training to increase competencies in workplace relationship skills.

GUIDELINES FOR A ZERO-TOLERANCE DISCRIMINATION AND HARASSMENT POLICY

The specific steps taken in a human rights malpractice prevention program will vary from company to company and so will the prevailing attitude surrounding the program. That is, the zero tolerance discrimination and harassment policy may be viewed as a human rights malpractice prevention program in its beginnings. As it takes hold, however, and these behaviors become the accepted and standard norm, they will be seen merely as the ways and means we go about in establishing good working relationships.

The following basic elements should be present in establishing the discrimination and harassment zero tolerance policy:

- A written policy;
- An ongoing employee orientation and education program;
- A complaint procedure;
- An accountability procedure; and
- An appeals process.

A Written Policy

As a preventive measure, each employer should adopt a clear, written policy. The policy should be part of the company's mission and vision statements, and it should be posted in a prominent location in the workplace. All members of the workforce should be advised of it.

The policy should include, at a minimum, the following elements:

- *Caveat*: Discrimination and harassment are illegal under state and federal law.
- *Mission Statement*: Discrimination and harassment are contrary to the policies and practices of the company. Infraction will not be tolerated and discipline of unlawful behavior will be immediate.
- *Examples:* Specific examples of the types of behaviors prohibited.
- *Instructions:* Step-by-step instructions on how individuals are to report discrimination and harassment practices to the appropriate supervisor or other members of management.
- *Commitment Statement:* All discrimination and harassment complaints will be investigated promptly and thoroughly, and anyone found guilty of discrimination and harassment will be disciplined accordingly.
- *Discipline Procedures:* Methods of discipline should be spelled out clearly.
- *Consequences:* As with all jurisprudence, consequence should relate directly to the misconduct cited and not be left up to individual interpretation or whim.

- *Audit:* A semi-annual internal audit of the policy's process should be made by professional outside auditors.

An Ongoing Employment Orientation and Education Program

Each employer should offer all employees a mandatory orientation and education program defining and delineating the company's discrimination and harassment policy. This program should acquaint employees with conduct that is appropriate and acceptable and that which is not. Discipline measures to be applied should be spelled out.

A Complaint Procedure

The creation and implementation of a discrimination and harassment complaint investigation and resolution procedure are essential to the employer prevention program. The mere presentation of a discrimination and harassment policy statement, no matter how well worded or stringent, is of little value without a complaint investigation and resolution procedure to implement it. This means that a clearly defined process that will protect both the complainant and the accused must be part of this policy. Several options for reporting should be offered and should include both formal and informal channels.

An Accountability Procedure

Prompt, thorough, consistent investigation of all complaints is essential for deterring further inappropriate behavior and liability. A team of impartial investigators should be assigned to interview the accuser, the accused, and the witnesses.

Inappropriate behavior should be answered with swift, decisive action which clearly demonstrates that the behavior will not be tolerated. Appropriate discipline and mediation may include counseling and discharge in flagrant or repeat cases.

An Appeals Process

A process for appeal needs to be established for those who are charged. A reporting process needs to be implemented so that employees know the results of actions taken and how the charges have been resolved.

A report to the President and Congress of the United States by the U.S. Merit Systems Protection Board recommends that penalties against discrimination and harassment should be publicized and that employees should be encouraged to react assertively if they are discriminated against or harassed. Managers and supervisors should be firm and consistent in penalizing proven discriminators or harassers. Consistency should set the tone of this program. A sense of fair play should be understood. Organizations should diagnose the extent and seriousness of the malpractice within their own organizations in order to know what kinds of solutions are appropriate and where resources should be concentrated. [4]

GUIDELINES FOR BASIC WORKPLACE BEHAVIOR STANDARDS

Companies faced with survival in today's fiercely competitive world must integrate diverse individuals into the work culture. Effective interaction between diverse employees is essential. Establishing proactive behavior standards expected of all employees supports that effort. It also helps employees understand needed areas of growth.

While designing and developing the company's basic workplace behavior standards, we ask ourselves and others in our organization, the following questions:

- How will our organization be different as a result of these behavior standards?
- What will people need to learn to comply with these standards?
- How will this information be provided?
- How will employees interact differently?
- How will the company's operational results be affected?
- How will we know when we have succeeded?

As we develop our company's basic workplace behavior standards, check to see if we:

- Focus on changing ineffective workplace behavior, not changing personal values and belief systems.
- Respect individuality and what each person brings to the workplace.
- Focus on individual empowerment.
- Appreciate individual abilities, talents, and skills.
- Share an organizational destination and a common sense of purpose between employer and employee.
- Offer accurate workforce behavior appraisal to all employees.
- Foster needed professional relationship skills training and development programs for all supervisors as well as for employees.

GUIDELINES FOR WORKPLACE RELATIONSHIP SKILLS DEVELOPMENT

This book presents an overview of managing our MindTalk,™ the Workplace Relationships Skills ToolKit,™ along with tables in the Appendix for individual, group, and/or team self study.

NOTES FOR LEADERS AND MANAGERS

The solution that we have provided for the workplace dilemma includes a process of company-wide culture change. Any culture change takes a lengthy period of time—not weeks or months, but years for the change to be fully implemented. Therefore, we cannot emphasize enough the importance of beginning immediately to put this solution into place, with the intent to end discrimination and harassment practices in our workplaces. A "do it now" attitude is needed, one that reflects a sense of urgency and immediacy.

As leaders, our employees look to us to lead the commitment toward eliminating discrimination and harassment practices throughout our companies. They expect us to march at the head of the parade and become a prime example of zero tolerance compliance. They will evaluate how well we uphold the company's basic interaction standards and the level of our workplace relationship skills. They expect near mastery level skills from us. They will look to see if our enthusiasm for this healthy human rights program is genuine; it won't work if we grudgingly comply. It is important to make the zero tolerance policy visible at every turn.

Employees need us to lead them away from historically worn-out ways—the misguided cultural patterns of the past that have damaged their ability to relate effectively with one another. Keep them informed. Let them know everything there is to know about implementing the zero tolerance discrimination and harassment policy. Tell them the logic, the rationale, behind the company's decision to eliminate these degrading practices and how this decision will change the company's formal and informal culture. Give them an airtight case, based on hard facts, about the diversity of the marketplace and the debilitating and costly effects of discrimination and harassment on the firm's competitive positioning.

Culture change needs lots of public relations. Talk about the change process at every possible opportunity—in meetings, through memos, presentations, company publications, and the casual give-and-take of everyday conversation and business transaction. They expect us as their leaders to send a clear and consistent message that breaks through all barriers and helps them break out of existing bad practices. [5]

As company managers, we are expected to produce tangible payoffs as a part of the solution to the workplace dilemma. The tangible payoffs for making this culture change are the number of employees retained, decreases in sick leave, higher employee productivity, customer satisfaction, and increased profits. It is important to make those successes known to our company employees in order to stimulate further development. Encourage growth, encourage change in every possible way.

We need to teach our people new workplace relationship skills. This training builds confidence, competencies, and willingness to change. Give employees techniques—position them to contribute. The more employees feel like they are contributing, the more they are willing to change. The more they believe their contributions are valued, the more they will be willing to try new things. [6]

If a zero tolerance discrimination and harassment policy designed by our company is not enforced, it will fail. When the employees realize the organizational culture is changing and that the zero tolerance policy has real teeth and that each employee will be held accountable for inappropriate behaviors, the workplace will go on red alert. So wave that red flag. Get everyone's attention. Set the company's standards high, so high that they challenge workers to reach for mastery level workplace relationship skills. Give individuals personal responsibility for transforming their workplace relationships. Let them know that they play an important part in the firm's competitive position.

Resistance is a normal part of the culture change process; so expect it, but don't let it stop the process. The transition period is one of high uncertainty, and if the uncertain energy is unmanaged, employees will retreat to their former habits and describe the experience as another meaningless "flavor of the month" change. So keep the heat on. Send out clear signals on how we want employees to behave. Don't exclude anyone, because those excluded will become more resistant and apathetic. Instead, increase our expectations. Reward employees for their successes. Let them know that the company culture matters and that they matter.

Penalize inappropriate behavior through swift, decisive action which clearly demonstrates discrimination and harassment behaviors are no longer tolerated. Take a firm stand. Leave no confusion as to what is expected. Don't settle for less.

SUMMARY

Although the implementation of the solution to the workplace dilemma might appear simple at first glance, we do not want to understate the effort involved or the systemic changes which are required. It is extremely important that the zero tolerance policy be outlined and emphasized, the workplace behavior standards be established early in the change process, and that a workplace relationship skills development program be implemented to educate managers and workers on how to avoid discrimination and harassment behaviors.

This simple and effective process has the power to enhance employer and employee work relationships. Productivity will be improved, customer satisfaction will be stimulated, and bottom-line profits increased.

NOTES

1. "Ending the Workplace Diversity Wars," Stephen Paskoff, *Training,* August 1996, p. 46.

2. "Jury Awards $50 Million in Wal-Mart Harassment," National Law Journal Staff and Associated Press Reporters, *The National Law Journal*, Vol. 17, No. 45, July 10, 1995.

3. "Insurers Join the Effort to Tackle Discrimination," *Wall Street Journal,* March 5, 1997.

4. Revised from the U.S. Merit System's Protection Board Report on Sexual Harassment in the Federal Workplace, October 1995.

5. "Diversity and Upward Mobility Obstacles Persist," Diversity Consultants for Towers Perrin, *Working Age,* Vol. 11, No. 3, September/October 1995.

6. The style of implementation that we recommend for organizations parallels the thrust advocated by Price Pritchert and Ron Pound in their *Handbook for Managers: High Velocity Culture Change,* 1993.

9

Benefits to Organizations

INTRODUCTION

Managing differences and avoiding discrimination and harassment costs are high-stake business issues. Workers who are unable or unwilling to function cooperatively hurt productivity, depress morale, and impede the achievement of corporate goals, causing an atmosphere that is ripe for discrimination and harassment lawsuits with multimillion dollar penalties. The need for a behavior change has surfaced as management's top priority. It has become the standard that determines company survival. Its purpose is to prevent corporate and personal loss and enhance the organization's ability to meet its business goals. [1]

The solution to the workplace dilemma offers significant benefits to organizations in the ability to: (1) Keep and/or gain market share; (2) Recruit and retain the best workers; (3) Increase employee productivity, profitability, creativity, innovation, and problem-solving abilities; and (4) Reduce legal costs.

KEEP AND/OR GAIN MARKET SHARE

Changing demographics in a global market is the current and future reality. This results in a consumer market for goods and services that is increasingly more diverse. Whether or not a company will hold its market share in the present global economy will depend on its ability to appeal to a diverse customer base and at the same time maintain an equally diverse employee pool. Organizations which hire from a diverse talent pool have a better understanding of their customers' needs and are better equipped to appeal to a more diverse customer market. This offers companies the opportunity to appeal to multicultural customers on the national level and tap into additional markets created by the increased spending power of African Americans, Hispanics and

Asian Americans. *The Diversity Marketing Outlook*, a Seattle magazine published by Barbara Deane, states that the annual purchasing power of African Americans is $400 billion, Hispanics is $235 billion, and Asian Americans is $150 billion. [2]

Additionally, public officials come from a variety of multicultural backgrounds and exert influence over factors that determine how well an organization produces and markets its goods and services. Those who hold public office and represent such diverse origins as African American, Hispanic, Asian American and other people of color are now making decisions about what taxes, advertising options, and fees any given organization may charge. Organizational leaders need the goodwill and support from people of many diverse cultures.

Customers in such a diverse marketplace have the expectation that a zero tolerance policy against discrimination and harassment will be enforced and the company's employees will have a high level of workplace relationship skills. Organizations no longer have the option of ignoring these emerging markets; they are essential in order to retain and gain market share for a company's goods and services. It is a sound business principle to eradicate harassment and discrimination.

RECRUIT AND RETAIN THE BEST WORKERS

White women, native-born people of color, and immigrants will increasingly dominate the U.S. workforce of the future. By the year 2000, white men will make up less than 38 percent of this new workforce. [3]

In the face of broad demographic changes, it becomes necessary for organizations to accommodate the enormity of this change or go under. Companies must be able to compete for the best workers. Organizations that do not recognize the need to cultivate and utilize the talents of their entire staff risk losing their competitive edge.

Bottom-line savings could come from the reduction of the high turnover rate among minorities and women employees alone. Continually hiring, training, and developing new people is expensive. Studies show that organizations now spend anywhere from $30,000 to $60,000 to recruit a university graduate. New recruits, once hired, must be trained, which can take anywhere from a few days to several months. Companies may spend up to $100,000 to recruit, train, and compensate a new employee; thus losing ten workers could mean losing up to a million dollars. [4]

Data from the U.S. Department of Labor show that turnover and absenteeism are higher among women and non-white men than they are for white males. Overall turnover rates for blacks in the U.S. workforce is 40 percent higher than for whites. Corning Inc. recently reported that during the period 1980-1987, turnover among women in professional jobs was double that of men and the turnover rates among blacks were 2.5 times those of whites. A two-to-one ratio in the turnover of women to men was also cited by Falice Schwartz in her article on multiple career tracks for women in management. Finally, a recent study of absenteeism rates in the U.S. workforce shows the rates for women are 58 percent higher than that for men. [5]

Many companies view their human resources as an expense rather than an asset—an element that is expendable and perhaps discarded when the skills possessed becomes obsolete. When human resources are viewed as an asset, companies enhance individual value through training and human development and ensure continued contribution to the organization. This not only decreases employee turnover, it also increases productivity and market share.

Providing a workplace free of the debilitating effects of discrimination and harassment is a critical issue and highlights the need to manage the company's most valuable asset and resource more carefully. That asset is the irreplaceable human being, a factor we sometimes forget. In the face of today's broad-based demographic changes, organizations that do not recognize the need to cultivate and utilize the talents of all human beings in their employ risk losing their competitive edge. [6]

INCREASE EMPLOYEE PRODUCTIVITY, PROFITABILITY, CREATIVITY, INNOVATION, AND PROBLEM-SOLVING ABILITIES

How individuals behave within their organization influences their individual career experiences and, in turn, affects the outcome or history of the organization.

The quality of employee's work-related relationships and whom they relate to within the workplace affects how they feel about their work and employer. In many organizations, these feelings, which translate into employee morale and satisfaction, are directly related to identity groups. How well the gender, race, or ethnic group that an individual relates to is treated affects both the individual and the organization.

How well a person performs on the job, and how that is measured by such things as job performance ratings, is affected by how the individual is treated by his or her supervisors and peers. This also may be related to group identities. In turn, the outcome of the individual impacts organizational effectiveness measures such as work quality, productivity, absenteeism, and turnover. Thus, how the lowest level worker is treated either limits or enhances the potential of the highest worker and, in turn, alters positively or negatively the company's progress.

For profit-making organizations, an employee's ability to function productively translates into profitability and market share. The interpersonal aspects of the company's cultural climate directly impact organizational performance. Specifically, the amount of discrimination and harassment of minority groups will impact factors such as creativity, problem-solving, and interorganizational communications. How well an organization treats its employees eventually determines the well-being of the organization at large and measures its failure or success.

What people believe about their opportunities in the work environment affects their work outcomes. In a recent study illustrating the relevance of individual perceptions to work outcomes, it was found that employees' perceptions of being valued by an organization had a significant effect on their consciousness, job involvement, and innovativeness. [7]

The sense of being considered valuable as an employee is influenced by cultural differences. Because of stereotyping, ethnocentrism, discounting, and prejudice, members of minority groups feel less valued.

Taylor Cox found in his studies that non-majority group members are more likely to be aware of the effects of group membership than majority group members. White women were nearly three times as likely as white men to say that being a man was an important factor in being promoted to senior positions. Non-whites (both men and women) were three times as likely to say that race was an important factor. Stereotyping, discrimination, and harassment behaviors tend to adversely affect the individual outcomes of persons in the targeted groups. Members of the favored majority group, be it race or gender, seldom feel that identification with the group is to their advantage. The fact that majority members often remain oblivious to the problem is a major reason that discrimination and harassment continue to exist. Members of the non-favored race or gender group however, always identify with their group. Malpractice targeted at minority subgroups hampers communications. This reduces the quality of the relationship between subgroups and managers. When breakdown happens, it diminishes the creativity and problem-solving abilities of everyone, especially the targeted groups. [8]

Enhancing creativity and problem-solving should be the prime concern of organizational leaders. Taking a stand by becoming a positive force in the fight for equitable and fair human rights practices can and should be a powerful incentive to stay on the job. As the number of high-performing women and minority managers increases, others will be inspired to stay and strive to reach higher levels. As this happens, positive change in the systemic culture of the organization will result.

The outcome will be greater productivity from all employees who enjoy coming to work. Employees who are relaxed instead of defensive or stressed in their work setting, and who are happy to be working because they feel valued and successful as individuals, make organizations productive and profitable.

REDUCE LEGAL COSTS

We detailed earlier the huge amounts organizations have paid to settle suits brought against them for discrimination and harassment practices. These examples, however, do not indicate the additional high legal and administrative expenses that organizations pay to defend themselves against all charges, many

of which are settled for undisclosed amounts out of court. Consider the multi-
tude of hidden expenses caused by the disruption of business that results from a
legal suit against a company. It is estimated that the actual cost to an organization is three to four times the amount of the settlement itself. Since 1991, the
number of civil rights employment suits filed in U.S. district courts has
increased 127 percent to 19,059 in 1995. [9]

Common sense dictates that the astronomical cost of discrimination and
harassment litigation payoffs alone would be ample reason for organizations to
develop a zero tolerance policy for discrimination and harassment.

NOTES

1. "End of Diversity Wars," Stephen Paskoff, *Training*, August 1996, p. 47.

2. *Diversity Marketing Outlook*, Barbara Deane, October 1996.

3. *Workforce 2000, Today: A Bottom-Line concern; Making Full Use of the Nation's
Human Capital*, Labor Department, 1995.

4. "Diversity: The Key to Quality Business," John E. Cleghorn, President and CEO,
Royal Bank of Canada, *Vital Speeches of the Day*, Vol. 14, No. 7, January 15, 1993.

5. *Cultural Diversity in Organizations: Theory Research, & Practice*, Taylor Cox, Jr.,
1993.

6. "You're on Your Own, Training, Employability, and the New Employment
Contract," Bob Filipczak, *Training*, January 1995, p. 34.

7. *Cultural Diversity in Organizations: Theory, Research & Practice*, Taylor Cox, Jr.,
1993.

8. Ibid.

9. "Diversity's Double-Edged Sword. It Can Expand Markets, but also Split Workforces," *Investors Business Daily*, February 20, 1997

10

The Window to the Future

INTRODUCTION

One novelty of the late twentieth century is that everything has come loose. This means that most people face a far wider range of choice than ever before. The need to deal with diversity and uncertainty has grown enormously. Author Charles Handy calls this the Age of Diversity.

The 1990s have been years of dramatic change. This change is felt on the social, economic, technological, demographic, cultural, and organizational front on a massive scale. Individual workers are profoundly affected. Their thoughts, feelings, and behaviors are in a state of confusion and chaos because of this dramatic change in the workplace. "A formula driving the future of work," Handy goes on to say, "is $1/2 \times 2 = 3$, which represents the pressure on organizations to use half as many people, paid twice as well, to produce three times as much." [1]

Here are areas that contribute to a work environment where it appears that everything has come loose:

- The changing workplace;
- The questionable future of affirmative action;
- Scaling back diversity programs;
- Organizational restructuring;
- The challenge of employability;
- Employer and employee covenants transformed;
- Entrepreneurial ventures; and
- The window to the future.

A CHANGING WORKPLACE

Restructuring of company hierarchies through mergers, acquisitions, and downsizing has changed historical contracts between employer and employee. Gone are the days when career planning was considered the domain of personnel and training functions within the organization. Entitlements are a thing of the past. Today's employee faces a future in which career choices are matters of individual choice. Most often these choices are made without the guidance and mentoring counted on as part of the work-a-day world by employees of the past.

The radical changes within U.S. organizations are driven by such powerful forces as:

- The new and emerging technology which changes the way people communicate;
- Global markets that raise the demand for improved products and services;
- The shift to a service orientation rather than an industrial product orientation;
- Employees who are changing their values, norms, and attitudes about work;
- The shift from a manufacturing-based economy to a knowledge-based economy;
- The downsizing, rightsizing, and merging in most U.S. organizations causing massive layoffs;
- The changing role and power of the unions;
- Industries moving to Third World countries for less expensive workers;
- A more diverse customer and employee base; and
- An aging workforce.

THE QUESTIONABLE FUTURE OF AFFIRMATIVE ACTION

The changing political climate, including recent Supreme Court decisions limiting the use of affirmative action in education, has convinced the corporate male that the high water mark of affirmative action has passed. [2] A recent *Wall Street Journal* article stated that the power-endowed corporate male is fighting back. [3] With downsizing and the fact that there are a lot of previously powerful corporate males out of careers and looking for work, there is now more overt concern about women and minorities competing for what white males territorially consider their jobs.

According to Mr. Sussman, a former consultant for Digital Equipment Corporation, more than 70 percent of the buyouts in Digital plants have been taken by women and blacks. Many women and minorities felt frustrated during the beginning of their progress up the corporate ladder. Now, however, the company states that the overall number of women and minority employees fell during downsizing, but that the number of women and minorities in senior management actually increased. [4]

Terrance Osley of AlliedSignal, Inc., in Morristown, New Jersey, reports that recent promotions in the financial field have all gone to white men.

A lot of the older regime is about to retire, and the baton is being passed not just to men but to younger white men. [5]

On the other hand, as mammoth companies like AT&T and Eastman Kodak trim their workforces and in that process remove tiers of veteran employees, age discrimination suits by displaced males are beginning to outnumber sex discrimination suits. Castoff male middle managers who once commanded high salaries are particularly prone to sue because they have more to gain by pursuing lost wages. Labor and legal experts say that much of the litigation could be avoided if the company had presented employees with options rather than arbitrarily throwing them out the door.

SCALING BACK DIVERSITY PROGRAMS

Many companies are soft-pedaling or scaling back diversity programs in response to male backlash. "Diversity training is really a non-issue," says John McNamara of AT&T. "There doesn't seem to be the same emphasis as there used to be to force people to enter diversity training programs." [6]

Equity Institute, considered instrumental in putting diversity issues on the national agenda, is closing for lack of funding. This institute trained thousands of trainers who played major roles in the historical diversity training movement. As a non-profit organization, it was dependent on donors to keep its doors open and when interest lagged, financial backing disappeared. [7] The organization was told its work was too controversial. In our opinion, diversity training failed because its focus offered no tangible results; nor did it seek resolution. That is, by focusing on differences rather than how to work with those that are different, diversity training raised issues, but did not take the necessary action to resolve conflict.

ORGANIZATIONAL RESTRUCTURING

In 1993, there were 615,000 announced corporate layoffs, 510,000 in 1994 and 440,000 in 1995. About 75 percent of those outplaced got new jobs, 14 percent retired, and 11 percent were unemployed after being fired, according to the Department of Labor. These layoffs take place through downsizing, right-sizing, mergers, and divestitures in U.S. organizations. [8] As a result, the average American worker is becoming increasingly anxious, states Edward Luttwak, author of *The Endangered American Dream*. "An unprecedented sense of personal economic insecurity has suddenly become the central phenomena of American life. This is true not only for that endangered species of corporate middlemen but for virtually all working Americans." Job security is a thing of the past. Recognition of this fact now permeates the already troubled workplace culture, thus increasing the levels of employee anxiety and discontent even further. [9]

A 1991 survey of the 4,500 largest companies in the United States conducted by *Fortune* magazine and the Wyatt Company, a consulting firm, revealed that 86 percent of U.S. organizations had downsized in the previous five years and most companies expected to downsize again. [10]

THE CHALLENGE OF EMPLOYABILITY

Since 1970, plant closings and corporate downsizing have displaced approximately two million workers a year. To be employable in the late 1990s and beyond, it is imperative that each person learn self-management and self-reliance skills. To find work, it is crucial that all workers develop the ability, skills, and tools to:

- Stay abreast of the myriad trends affecting their industry, their company, their department, and their work roles;
- Evaluate and manage their present work environment;
- Self-start;
- Become lifetime learners;
- Have and update broad, competitive skill sets;
- Be innovative and creative;
- Be entrepreneurial;
- Manage their own Mindtalk™;
- Become proficient in their own workplace relations management;
- Be effective communicators by developing high skill levels in listening, conflict resolution, generating feedback and negotiation;
- Build an alliance with their employer as co-creators in their company's success; and
- Market and sell themselves effectively.

To compete in today's labor market, employees must continuously seek ways of self-improvement. To prepare themselves adequately, they must become "market smart" by understanding what job skills and behavior skills will be needed in the future. They must learn to effectively manage themselves personally and professionally.

EMPLOYER/EMPLOYEE COVENANTS TRANSFORMED

As companies and employees struggle to adapt to new technologies, the information explosion, and a global economy that shifts on an almost daily basis, employee and employer relationships are being completely transformed. Sometimes this transforming process happens relatively smoothly as companies guide their employees to support a vision or business plan. At other times, the shifts occur radically and painfully as companies arbitrarily cut hundreds of thousands of jobs.

Established workplace covenants which formed the cultural guidelines and norms traditionally governing professional policies, processes, and relationships of the past are no longer in place. Those covenants, reflecting accepted norms of society, set in place specific expectations for employees and employers alike. While not stated explicitly, it was understood that if employees were loyal, worked hard, and did good work, they would be entitled to lifetime employment. Most companies of today have broken that fundamental rule. So have young employees who have no plans to stick around for the "gold watch."

Just as in the past when ground rules of mutual trust remained unspoken, most of what is happening today goes unsaid. Many other historical covenants related to benefits, wages, and seniority are being violated as well. These actions, even in their mildest form, strain relationships. More apparent, however, is the extremely damaging climate of distrust and uncertainty emerging between employers and employees. The world of work, once housed in a climate of mutual trust, is slowly being overrun by a corrosive atmosphere of distrust. Employees are expected to behave naturally in the midst of this chaos and perform to full capacity, in spite of being confused by the unrealistic expectation levels required of them or the mixed messages they are receiving.

New covenants, just beginning to appear on the horizon, are not yet clearly defined. Both the companies and the individuals who work for them are caught in the chaos of transition. What is clear amid all of the confusion, however, is that these new covenants, as well as the workplace of the future, will look unlike anything ever witnessed before. Moreover, it is becoming increasingly clear that these new covenants will be based upon individual skills, knowledge, and workplace relationship skills, with less emphasis on age, sex, or other traditionally limiting criteria. As employers are being forced to change their workplace covenants, employees must learn to adjust. What they must adjust to is a complete, radical change in their performance expectation levels. Some of the changes in skill levels facing the individual employee are:

- Instead of loyalty, commitment to, and longevity with an employer, competence is based upon task completion and accountability;
- Instead of one primary skill, multiple skills sets, both technical and interpersonal, are being sought;
- Instead of entitlements, employers are expecting employees to be self-reliant;
- Instead of one career with life-long employment in one company, employees may expect multiple careers in a variety of companies and industries; and
- Instead of an emphasis on jobs and positions, employers will be looking for skills, knowledge, added value, relationship skills, and performance results.

Many organizations are re-recruiting their workforce. Employees are being required to reapply for their own positions. During this restructuring process, millions of employees have left, or will soon be leaving companies through downsizing, rightsizing, and layoffs. For most of these workers, this is the time for serious assessment of their employability and reassessment of the realities they face in the changing workplace. It is a time of serious reflection and introspection. For many, it has become the time to develop self-reliance skills, especially if their livelihood becomes imperiled through new job descriptions that find them no longer qualified for the position they hold because the skills level required for the position they hold has been changed without their knowing it.

Given these odds, thousands of laid-off workers have chosen entrepreneurial ventures and are building their own, often home-based, businesses. Those remaining in or returning to the workplace realize that they also must be self-reliant and have an intrapreneurial (entrepreneuring inside the company) mind-set.

As reality sets in, employees from all levels are slowly beginning to understand that:

- Job security is a thing of the past;
- Responsibility for employability is shifting from the company to the individual;
- Individuals must continually and actively market themselves to their company;
- Each individual must take it upon himself or herself to access tools and services needed to assist them in being prepared for all the changing conditions in the workplace; and
- The employee needs more information about the company's business direction and skills.

In turn, managers are beginning to realize that they must:

- Organize and redefine their work processes with a base of fewer full-time, salaried and traditional employees, with less hierarchical organization structures, and more decentralized control systems; and
- Manage employees who think of themselves as independent business resources and entertain the idea of employing the independent contractor.

Driven by this quest to improve bottom-line profits, organizations are being forced to create new structures such as self-managed and cross-functional teams, strategic alliances, and partnerships. Even former competitors are creating business alliances. Additionally, companies everywhere are finding less expansive alternatives to full-time jobs by outsourcing, brokering, and contracting. This alone has accelerated the explosion of the individually owned enterprise—the home-based business.

ENTREPRENEURIAL VENTURES

The U.S. Labor Department states that a growing share of American workers, currently 19.8 percent of the workforce or more than 24 million workers, have established income-generating resources different from the traditional ongoing relationship with a single employer. Entrepreneurial ventures, home businesses, and business consulting firms are a few of the options that displaced employees choose.

To meet the demands of this accelerating change, both companies and their workers are being forced to revise the traditional ways in which employees and employers function together. The backlash of this phenomenon is the creation of an independent employee who is, in nature and habit, a startling contrast to the dependent employee of the past, who was willing to put up with anything so long as the job remained secure. This is challenging employers and employees alike to rethink their communication procedures. It is becoming increasingly clear that both parties must revise their thinking and habit patterns. New skills are needed to meet future business challenges. Employer and employee alike must ask, "What knowledge and skill sets do I need to manage these changing roles and changing relationships in these changing times?"

Americans used to think in terms of a social contract, and even a generation ago that contract was as good as a handshake. Today the strength of that relationship is based upon a skills needs package whereby both employers and employees see one another as mutual providers. New arrangements are based upon knowledge, skill, task completion, accountability, and workplace relationship skills and are interdependent, rather than dependent.

THE WINDOW TO THE FUTURE

The future of business in a global economy will rest upon employees being able to think and act across ethnic, cultural, and linguistic lines with informed grace. The employee of the future can look forward to moving easily among different countries, currencies, languages, and customs. Entrance into the workforce will create this avenue for each person as new doors open to them. Employees of the future will be global citizens who are comfortable living and working anywhere.

The realities of the workforce in the next decade are as multicultural as the reality of previous decades was monocultural. Differences among races, nations, and cultures, with their various histories, are at least as profound and as durable as their similarities. The ability to come to terms with differences in nationality, race, ethnicity, gender, disability, and workplace relationships will be a critical predictor of each individual's economic success in the next century.

The workplace and business markets of the future will be made up of native-born people of color and immigrants from Third World countries. As U.S. businesses enter this global marketplace, they will have to integrate foreign employees into their organizations, not only on foreign soil but also in America. Ethnicity and gender issues will continue to need resolution, and cultural and language issues will become increasingly complex. Companies must learn to utilize fully their potential as workers and consumers in order to survive and prosper in the coming decades. U.S. companies must learn to deal with an even more diverse workforce. They must develop short-term and long-term plans to manage this new workforce effectively. If not, American business will lose out to its competition.

Additionally, the U.S. workforce is destined to grow slightly faster in the 1990s than it did during the 1980s. The Bureau of Labor Statistics projects annual increases in employment of 1.5 percent between 1992 and 2005, compared with 1.4 percent between 1979 and 1992. This translates into the addition of 16 million jobs and a total civilian employment of more than 147 million by 2005. [11]

Carolyn Corbin's trend analysis projects that, by the year 2005, tapping the power of a diverse workforce will bring about a very different configuration. Seventy percent of all employees will be contract, temporary, or portfolio workers. Except for core groups in the organization, permanent employment will be nonexistent. [12] In this same vein, Peter Drucker predicts that by the year 2010, the largest corporations will have no more than 200 permanent employees. [13] This places the responsibility for economic survival directly on the individual worker.

"Any company of significant size that isn't doing business internationally will not be in existence in ten years," states Dr. James Crupi in a 1995 keynote address to an international business association. [14] Dr. Crupi is president of Strategic Leadership Solutions, advisor to Fortune 500 company executives and to President Clinton. He goes on to describe how this will change the roles and behaviors of worldwide organizations and their workers. With advanced technology, companies that develop major international business projects and/or products will need to be capable of employing individuals from any geographical location, representing any nationality in the world.

This trend is only going to increase in the future. Companies ranging from General Motors to IBM and Citibank already have branches of their companies overseas producing goods "cheaper, faster, and better." Microsoft, Boeing, and Nordstrom's find that they save as much as 40 percent by employing overseas software services. [15] These companies are required to communicate effectively with fellow employees of their global counterparts. Those who find themselves in places of employment where there are no common areas except shared skills, and where nearly everyone stems from a different racial, ethnic, or cultural background, will not be able to cope unless they have highly developed workplace relationship skills. Employees and/or employers that continue to harbor discrimination and harassment behaviors toward those who are different will not succeed.

Emerging visions of this new work world mark the dawn of a new era of history. The approaches which worked well in the past are proving counterproductive and must be discarded. Futurist Robert Theobald states that there are two dominant trends in the future. They are long-term thinking and long-term relationships. Long-term relationships are not built in an atmosphere that harbors discrimination and harassment. [16] Nicholas Negropante, director of Media Lab at the Massachusetts Institute of Technology, predicts that the Internet will have more than one billion users by the year 2000. [17] As we move into the twenty-first century, digital literacy will become a necessary and essential skill. Employees will be hired on a skills match basis, often without the benefit of a personal interview. This type of technology will make new demands on both employers and employees. Industry will be more interested in the skilled, flexible worker who is able to take advantage of new technology than it will be in the candidate's race or gender.

The Internet provides worldwide intra- and inter-company connections, facilitating the exchange of electronic mail, bulletin-board items, and other data. The exchanges range from short messages to multi-million-byte transfers of photographs, software and other kinds of data. The Internet also connects companies and their customers. Products of the future will be sold and business will be transacted without buyer or seller meeting face-to-face. [18]

Within the next ten years, we will see significant shifts in how and where we work, the companies we work for and where we live. We will, in fact, have redefined our entire concept of work. New communication capabilities will make it far easier to stay in touch with friends and business acquaintances. Even small companies will have world-class information tools. This will create a corporate landscape in which a company's success depends less and less on its financial resources and more and more on its intellectual resources. Communications are the cutting edge. And good communications will be measured against interaction standards that depend entirely upon each individual's workplace relationship skills package.

Successful navigation through this new era requires the application of the solution to the workplace dilemma. We stand at the window to the future. We open this window wide to allow the winds of change and the power of co-responsibility to flow through and rid the workplace of discrimination and harassment practices.

NOTES

1. "Lies Ahead," *Training and Development,* January 1996, p. 77.
2. "That's No White Male," *Wall Street Journal,* September 5, 1996.
3. "White Men Shed Work Anxiety," *Wall Street Journal,* September 5, 1996.
4. "The Changing Workforce," *Seattle Times,* May 2, 1992.
5. "White Men Shed Work Anxiety," *Wall Street Journal,* September 5, 1996.
6. "White Men Shake Off that Losing Feeling on Affirmative Action," Jonathan Kaufman, *Wall Street Journal,* September 5, 1996.
7. Letter written by Joan Steineau Lester, executive director, Equity Institute, July 31, 1996.
8. "The Future of Work," Rick Feller, *Vocational Educational Journal,* April 1996, p. 27.
9. A quote from *The Endangered American Dream* in "Global Competition is at the Heart of the Dispute," *Seattle Times,* October 8, 1995.
10. "You're on Your Own: Training, Employability, and the New Employment Contract," Bob Filipczak, *Training,* January 1995, p. 32.
11. Ibid.

12. *Conquering Corporate Codependence: Lifeskills for Making It Within or Without the Corporation,* Carolyn Corbin, with Gene Busnar, 1993.

13. *Innovation and Entrepreneurship: Practices and Principles,* Peter E. Drucker, 1985.

14. "Forces Shaping the Future: Laying the Groundwork for Global Change," James Crupi, Ph.D, video of keynote speech to an international real estate association, 1995.

15. "A Byte of India," Jennifer Pjorhus, *Seattle Times,* September 15, 1996.

16. *The Rapids of Change: Social Entrepreneurship in Turbulent Times,* Robert Theobald, 1987, p. 11.

17. "What Lies Ahead," Warren Bennis, *Training and Development,* January 1996, p. 78.

18. "The Road Lies Ahead," Bill Gates, *Working Women,* September 1996, p. 9.

Appendix

Resources for Increasing
Workplace Relationship Skills,
Including the
Workplace Relationship Skills ToolKit™

Table A
Workplace Relationship Skills Continuum

Below are two lists of interaction descriptors that form a continuum of skill levels from a limiting level to a mastery level. One a scale of 1 to 5, place a check on the number that designates your present level of interacting.

Limiting Level_____to _____Mastery Level

Limiting Level	1	2	3	4	5	Mastery Level
Judgmental	1	2	3	4	5	Non-judgmental
Discounting	1	2	3	4	5	Respectful
Closed-minded	1	2	3	4	5	Transformational
Selective listener	1	2	3	4	5	Empathic listener
Insensitive	1	2	3	4	5	Compassionate
Impulsive	1	2	3	4	5	Self-controlled
Self-centered	1	2	3	4	5	Considers others
Denies emotions	1	2	3	4	5	Deals with emotions
Fear of change	1	2	3	4	5	Open to change
Defensive	1	2	3	4	5	Vulnerable
Afraid	1	2	3	4	5	Empowered
Exclusive	1	2	3	4	5	Free to choose
Discriminating	1	2	3	4	5	Open to difference
Segregated	1	2	3	4	5	Integrated
Stereotyping	1	2	3	4	5	Open-minded
TOTAL NUMBER	1	2	3	4	5	

If your score is less than 75, it would be helpful to you to increase your workplace relationship skills.

Table B
Internal Operating Committee (IOC) Members

The Boss, the rule maker	The Executive, the manager
The Caretaker, the helper	The Adult, the logical one
The Politician, the social one	The Employee, the worker
The Child, the feeling one	The Rebel, the rebellious one
The Mother, the nurturer	The Father, the authority
The Spiritual Advisor, the wise one	The Critic, the assessor
The Mentor, the knowledgeable one	The Friend, the sharer
The Dictator, the one who is always right	The Doubter, the negative one
The Brother, the competitor/the ally	The Sister, the ally/the competitor
The Healer, the pain killer	The Lover, the sweetheart
The Male, the masculine one	The Female, the feminine one
The Abuser, the aggressor	The Church, the rule maker

and many more.

Table C
Typical Conflicting Figures

Boss/Rebel	Employee/Dictator	Employee/Mother
Employee/Father	Dictator/Child	Female/Abuser
Child/Mother	Boss/Child	Male/Female

Table D
Examples of Closed-Filter Situations

Trauma	Depression	Fatigue
Stress	Hunger	Anger
Body chemical change	Pain	Threat

Table E
Examples of Open-Filter Situations

Safe	Nonjudgmental	Loved
Trusted	Listened to	Respected
Open	Free	Appreciated

Table F
Workplace Relationship Skills ToolKit™

By using the techniques below, which are contained in the Workplace Relationship Skills Toolkit,™ you can become your own coach, mentor, supervisor, teacher, or therapist.

- Increase Listening Skills;

- Interrupt and Reframe Negative MindTalk;™

- Interrupt and Control Negative Emotional Habit Patterns;

- Interrupt the Victimization Cycle;

- Understand the Communication Process

- Improve Conflict Management Skills; and

- Explode Relationship Myths.

Table G
Increase Listening Skills

1. Question your perceptions—be open to new perceptions.

2. Challenge clusters of perceptions about yourself and your listening skills.

3. Interrupt and reframe listening habit patterns.

4. Control Filters. Increase the fluidity of your filters through positive MindTalk.™

5. Notice when your attention has turned inward. Deliberately focus your eyes on the speaker and pay attention to the speaker's point of view.

6. Be conscious of being distracted and bring your focus back to the speaker.

7. Listen to understand the meaning as well as the emotions behind the message.

8. Ask for feedback from the speaker to validate your understanding.

Table H
Pain-to-Power Vocabulary Chart

Pain - - - - - - - - - - - to - - - - - - - - - Power	
I can't	I don't want to
I should	I could if I wanted to
It's not my fault	I am totally responsible
It's a problem	It's an opportunity
I'm never satisfied	I want to grow—learn
Life's a struggle	Life's an adventure
I hope	I know
If only	Next time
What will I do?	I can handle it
It's terrible	It's a learning experience

Table I
Interrupt and Reframe Negative MindTalk™

How to interrupt negative MindTalk.™

1. Choose to change—begin with small steps.

2. Focus attention on MindTalk.™ Notice the negative language and tone.

3. When feeling hurt, check to see if you are putting yourself down—are you describing yourself or something you did in a disparaging fashion. Write down the hurtful comments you have made about yourself to yourself and watch for repeated negative patterns in your MindTalk.™

4. Question perceptions and gather new information about the situation.

5. Challenge and expand your cluster of perceptions about yourself and others.

6. Identify and interrupt unconscious negative thought and mood habit patterns. Use your outside observer, your conscious mind, to deliberately bring these patterns into conscious awareness.

7. Control your filtering system by using your conscious mind to reframe the situation to more positive behavior.

8. Choose self-enhancing MindTalk,™ practice the change until it feels more natural.

9. Repeat self-affirming statements until they become your dominant habit pattern.

Table J
Interrupt and Control Negative Emotional Habit Patterns

1. Choose to change—begin with small steps.

2. Focus attention on your emotions and identify what you feel from moment to moment.

3. Keep a daily journal charting your emotions and reactions.

4. Identify the unconscious negative emotional reactions that stem from your habitual negative MindTalk™ and deliberately bring the thoughts and feelings into conscious awareness.

5. Question perceptions—gather new information about emotional reactions.

6. Challenge the cluster of perceptions about your emotional reactions and the emotional reactions of others.

7. Interrupt negative emotional habit patterns. Distract yourself from a constant focus on internal negative thoughts and feelings by deliberately focusing attention on something interesting outside of yourself, such as reading a novel, watching a movie, socializing, exercising, talking on the telephone to a friend, going to therapy, or having a special treat.

8. Manage the filtering system by using the conscious mind to reframe negative emotions as more positive thoughts, and your feelings will follow.

9. Choose self-enhancing MindTalk™ messages to soothe your emotional state. Practice the change until it feels more natural.

10. Practice relaxation methods and learn to meditate.

11. Repeat self-affirming statements until they become the dominant habit pattern.

Table K
Interrupt the Victimization Cycle

1. Question perceptions about yourself as victim, oppressor, or rescuer. Watch for clues that you are not taking responsibility for what you are saying, being, having, doing, or feeling.

2. Recognize that negative MindTalk™ fuels your involvement in the victimization cycle. Identify and relax parts that interfere with your choices.

3. Challenge clusters of perceptions regarding authority, acceptance, accountability, and responsibility. Allow perceptions to broaden and increase self-acceptance, and learn to pay attention to perceptions that foster acceptance and understanding of others.

4. Interrupt unconscious habit patterns of succumbing to the victimization cycle. Bring behaviors into conscious awareness—learn to take responsibility for your own behavior and make choices for yourself.

5. Examine what is gained by perceiving yourself as a victim, persecutor, or rescuer.

6. Control filters so they do not interfere with or obstruct the awareness of our interactions.

7. Ask for feedback from neutral parties to expand your perceptions.

8. Give yourself permission to stand up for your rights and the rights of others.

9. Review communication and assertiveness skills.

10. Determine what is wanted from relationships—take action to achieve goals that meet your needs.

Table L
Improve Conflict Management Skills: Behaviors That Escalate Conflict

1. Do not *minimize the problem:* When someone identifies a problem, the first thing to do is acknowledge it.   To make light of the problem through humor or sarcasm belittles others and makes them feel undervalued.

2. Do not *blame the other person:* Most problems are too complex to be caused totally by one person or one factor.

3. Do not *unload on the other person:* Bringing up a laundry list of past grievances only complicates the present conflict issue. Instead, bring up problems as they occur.

4. Do not *inflict low blows:* As we work with people, we begin to understand their sensitivities. Hitting one of these emotional touchy areas can escalate a conflict out of control and make it very difficult to regain lost ground.

5. Do not *manipulate the other person:* Using personal charm or approval to get someone to do something you want done without regard to the other person's needs or objections will only backfire.

6. Do not *use force:* This is the "I don't care what you want, do it my way, now!" approach.   If all you want is to get immediate action, it works, but this is demoralizing to the person and will not resolve the basic conflict.

Table M
Improve Conflict Management Skills: Behaviors That Resolve Conflict

1. If one member of the party needs to withdraw, that person must establish a time to return to the negotiating process.

2. Neither party will discount the opinions of the other person during the interaction.

3. Each participant will take responsibility for his or her own thoughts, feelings, and behaviors during the interaction. Both parties will use I-statements and include their feeling in their comments, such as "I feel hurt when you say . . . "

4. A specific length of time will be designated for each speaker to make his or her own point. The listening party will give the speaker full and undivided attention.

5. Each party will attempt to identify and emphasize areas of agreement. Each will look at conflict as a way to find a new and improved solution to the problem.

6. Each party will state his/her position tentatively, with the willingness to change his/her opinion if appropriate.

7. Each party will treat the other person and his/her ideas and opinions as equals.

8. Each party will express concern and support for the other party. It is important to demonstrate that we want to find a solution that benefits both parties.

Table N
Explode Relationship Myths

Myth #1:   My way of thinking is normal, and anyone who thinks differently is not normal.

Myth #2:   Most people feel the way I do.

Myth #3:   I can't change how I feel, think, and/or behave.

Myth #4:   My current behavior has nothing to do with my past experience.

Myth #5:   I believe that women usually overreact emotionally.

Myth #6:   I believe that men are generally unemotional and uncaring.

Myth #7:   You shouldn't feel the way you do.

Myth #8:   My behavior is based on common sense and logic. Therefore, I know I am right.

Myth #9:   If you cared about me, you would know what I want.

Myth #10: It is not my fault; you caused my pain.

Myth #11: I am not responsible for your inability to understand me.

Myth #12: I don't feel anything.

Myth #13: Not showing your feelings demonstrates that you are strong.

Myth #14: I can change you.

Myth #15: My interaction limitations were caused by my parents.

Myth #16: We can communicate easily and effectively.

Myth #17. Discrimination and harassment do not exist in the workplace.

Glossary

Able-bodied: Preferred term for describing a person without a disability; use instead of "normal," which should only be used to refer to statistical norms, etc.

Acculturation: True acculturation is a two-way street of changes and adaptations by both a new culture and an established one. This term is often misused, frequently implying the melting pot theory of giving up an old culture and becoming accepted by emulating the established (right) culture.

Affirmative action: A broad spectrum of measures and initiatives which are utilized to overcome the effects of past or present barriers to equal employment opportunity. These initiatives include training programs, recruitment, changes in promotion and layoff procedures, and the elimination of discriminating elements in an employer's selection criteria.

Assimilation: Becoming more like members of the dominant society.

Benchmark: A standard that is used measure the progress of an initiative or organization.

Bias: Partiality, a favorable or unfavorable feeling toward an individual or group.

Bisexuality: The term for a person whose same-gender and opposite-gender orientations are more or less equally intense. Some people, particularly young people, often self-identify as bisexual during a transition stage when they are in conflict with the demands of a hetrosexual society and their acknowledgment and acceptance of their homosexuality.

Change: An alteration, modification, correction, remodeling, switch, reformation, reconstruction; to make different, adjust, reorganize.

Collective: Group identification by race, sex, ethnicity, occupation, age, or combinations thereof. We are usually seen as part of a collective before we are perceived as individuals. A collective has both positive and negative associations. The negative associations often lead to stereotyping (i.e., using information and misinformation to judge everyone who belongs to a specific group or collective).

Competitive advantage: Qualities that makes a product more desirable than those offered by the competition.

Consultant: An individual (change agent) who is assisting an organization (client system) to become more effective. An external consultant is not a member of the system. An internal consultant is a member of the organization being assisted, but may or may not have a job title that reflects this.

Corporate culture: The pattern of values, beliefs, and expectations shared by organization members. It represents the taken-for-granted and shared assumptions that people make about how work is to be done and evaluated and how employees relate to each other and to others, such as suppliers, customers and government agencies.

Culture: Culture is the way of life—including values, beliefs, esthetic standards, verbal expression, patterns of thinking, behavioral norms, and styles of com-munication—which a group has developed to assure its survival in a particular physical and human environment.

Demography: The scientific study of human populations, primarily with respect to their size, composition and development. Study of the statistical characteristics of a population.

Denial: Repudiation, disclaimer, rejection, refutation, retraction, dismissal, renun-ciation, refusal to recognize, the cold shoulder, the brush-off. An example of denial would be to believe that the civil rights movement has taken care of discrimination.

Disability, disabled, physical disability: These terms are preferred over "handicap(ped)" to describe a permanent physical condition that interferes with a person's ability to do something independently—walk, see, hear, talk, dress, learn, lift, work, etc.

Discrimination: Treatment of a person or group (either intentional or unintentional) based on race, color, national origin, religion, sex, disability, or veteran's status.

Diversity: Differences among people or peoples reflected in a variety of forms, such as age, culture, disabilities, education, ethnicity, gender, language, politics, race, religion, sexual orientation, social class, and values.

Diversity training: Raising personal awareness about individual differences in the workplace and how these differences inhibit or enhance the way people work together or get work done. It provides education on compliance—Affirmative action and equal employment opportunity—and sexual harassment. The major emphasis is on race and gender issues.

Downsizing: Reducing the size of a company's workforce through layoffs, forced retirements, or attrition.

Effectiveness: Increasing competitiveness through efficiency, quality, and improved human relations.

Empowerment: Providing individuals or groups with the authority, responsibility, and tools to make decisions affecting them or their work.

Ethnic: Of or relating to people grouped according to a common racial, national, tribal, religious, linguistic, or cultural origin.

Ethnic pride: The celebration and maintenance of support of a cultural identity and its practices (not based on competition with other cultures).

Ethnicity: A sense of being different from other groups because of cultural tradition, ancestry, national origin, history, or religion.

Ethnocentrism: The belief that your culture is the best, to the exclusion of all other cultures. A proclivity for viewing members of one's own group as the center of the universe.

Facilitate: A process in which events are influenced and helped to happen.

Feminism: The principle that women should have political, economic, and social rights equal to those of men. The movement to win equal rights for women.

Gay: The term for same-gender sexual orientation. The term gay is preferred to homosexual because the latter implicitly emphasizes the sexual and diminishes the other aspects of gender orientation.

Gay man/male: Term for a man with a same-gender sexual orientation.

Glass ceiling: Artificial barriers that exist in the workplace and prevent or limit women and people of color from advancing to the upper levels of management.

Global corporations: Multinational corporations that sell the same product(s) in the same way throughout the world.

Handicap(ped): Often used as a synonym for "disability (disabled)." Increasingly, however, it is the preferred term for describing environmental conditions such as stairs, attitudes, or laws, etc., that inhibit a person's ability to function independently. For example, it would be appropriate to say that the stairs are a handicap for child in a wheel chair, not that the handicapped child could not use the stairs.

Harassment: To worry or torment, to tease, vex, irritate.

Harassment, sexual: Deliberate and/or repeated sexual or sex-based behavior that is not welcome, not asked for, and not returned.

Hierarchy: Pyramid organizational structure comprising top, middle and lower management.

Homophobia: Fear of or other emotional aversion to lesbians and gay men. Prejudice or bigotry toward lesbians and gay men.

Institutional racism: A variety of systems operating within an organization that involve attitudes, behaviors, and practices that subordinate persons or groups because of race or ethnic background.

Intrapreneurs: Individuals within an organization who act as though they are in business for themselves.

Lesbian: Term for a woman with same-gender sexual orientation.

Life-long Learning: Continuous learning from one's actual work and life experiences.

Managing Diversity: Creating an organizational environment that takes advantage of the different attributes of everyone—for both the good of the organization and the individual.

Melting pot: Blending of cultures, nationalities, and customs.

Mindset: Your personal viewpoint, formed from your cluster of perceptions.

MindTalk™: What we say to ourselves about ourselves and others inside our minds.

Monocultural: Lacking the ability to be culturally diverse.

Multicultural: The coexistence of many distinct cultures within a given context, such as workplace, school, community, or nation.

Paradigm: A set of rules and regulations that define boundaries. Strongly held paradigms act as filters that screen the way one views the world.

Pluralism: A system that includes individuals or groups differing in basic background experiences and cultures. It allows for the development of a common tradition, while preserving the right of each group to maintain its cultural heritage.

Politically correct (PC) language: A reference to terms used to describe individuals or groups that differ from the dominant group. Diversity trainers and multicultural specialists foster the use of terms that enhance rather than negate the individual or group.

Prejudice: To prejudge. Implies a preconceived idea, judgment, or opinion—usually an unfavorable one marked by suspicion, fear, intolerance or hatred—and directed toward a racial, religious, cultural, or ethnic group.

Quality assurance: A company-wide system of practices and procedures to assure that company products satisfy customers.

Racism: An assumption that there is an inherent purity and superiority of certain races and inferiority of others. It denotes any attitude, behavior, or institutional structure that subordinates persons or groups because of their race or ethnic background. Such practices can be intentional or unintentional.

Self-directed work team: A work group that has a clearly defined series of tasks and a clear boundary so that the group can be generally responsible for its own output and quality. Management has delegated to the self-directed work team the authority to plan, implement, control. and improve all work processes.

Self-esteem: How a person feels about herself or himself; pride in oneself. Self-esteem is linked to family traditions, language, social customs, economic background, and other aspects of one's cultural environment.

Sexual orientation: A term usually limited to reference homosexual, heterosexual, or bisexual behaviors.

Stereotypes: The belief that all people of a certain racial, ethnic, or cultural group are the same and behave in the same way.

Team building: A sequence of planned action designed to gather and analyze data on the functioning of a group and implement changes to increase its operating effectiveness.

Values: Values are subjective reactions to the world. They develop early in life through our direct experiences with people who are important, particularly parents. Values are resistant to change. They guide and mold options and behavior. They are internal definitions of what is good, right, and wrong.

Valuing diversity: Being able to work with a diverse group of people in a manner that enables all to reach their full potential in pursuit of organizational objectives.

Workplace relationship skills: These are the core skills needed for people to work more effectively and productively in a diverse workplace.

Workplace Relationship Skills ToolKit ™: A set of self-directed techniques that are essential to improving workplace relationship skills.

Selected Bibliography

Alessandera, Tony, Ph.D., and Phil Hunsaker, Ph.D. *Communicating at Work.* New York: A Fireside Book, 1993.

American Society for Training and Development (ASTD). *Resource Guide Workforce Diversity,* 1994.

Angelou, Maya. *Phenomenal Women: Four Poems Celebrating Women.* New York: Random House, 1994.

Bailyn, Lotte. *Breaking the Mold: Women, Men, and Time in the New Corporate World.* New York: The Free Press, A Division of Macmillan, Inc., 1993.

Bennis, Warren, and Patricia Ward Biederman. *Organizing Genius.* New York: Addison-Wesley Publishing, 1997.

Blank, Renee, and Sandra Slipp. *Voices of Diversity: Real People Talk About Problems and Solutions in a Workplace Where Everyone Is Not Alike.* New York: American Management Association, 1994.

Blank, Renee, and Sandra Slipp. *The White Male: An Endangered Species.* New York: American Management Association, 1994.

Bly, Robert. *Iron John.* New York: Addison-Wesley Publishing, 1990.

Boyett, Joseph H., and Henry P. Conn. *Workplace 2000: The Revolution Reshaping American Business.* New York: Dutton, published by the Penguin Group, 1991.

Bridges, William. *JobShift: How to Prosper in a Workplace Without Jobs.* New York: Addison-Wesley Publishing, 1994.

Bureau of National Affairs Employment Discrimination Report 1072. Washington, D.C., 1975.

Cannon, Margaret. *The Invisible Empire: Racism in Canada.* Vancouver, Canada: Random House of Canada, 1995.

Carnevale, Anthony Patrick, and Susan Carol Stone. *The American Mosaic: An In-Depth Report on the Future of Diversity at Work.* New York: McGraw-Hill, Inc., 1995.

Carter, Stephen L. *Reflections of an Affirmative Action Baby.* New York: Basic Books, 1991.

Caudron, Shari. "Training Can Damage Diversity Efforts." *Personnel Journal.* 1993.

Cavalli-Sforza, Luigi Luca, and Francesco Cavalli-Sforza. *The Great Human Diasporas: The History of Diversity and Evolution.* New York: Addison-Wesley Publishing, 1995.

Cleghorn, John E. "Diversity: The Key to Quality Business." *Vital Speeches of the Day.* Vol. 14, no.7, January 15, 1993.

Corbin, Carolyn, with Gene Busnar. *Conquering Corporate Codependence: Lifeskills for Making It Within or Without the Corporation.* Englewood Cliffs, New Jersey: Prentice-Hall, 1993.

Cornish, Edward, Editor. *The 1990's and Beyond.* Bethesda, Maryland: World Future Society, 1990.

Cose, Ellis. *The Range of a Privileged Class: Why are Middle-Class Blacks Angry? Why Should America Care?* New York: Harper Collins, 1993

Covey, Stephen R. *The 7 Habits of Highly Effective People: Powerful Lessons in Personal Change.* New York: A Fireside Book, published by Simon & Schuster, Inc., 1989.

Cox, Taylor, Jr. *Cultural Diversity in Organizations: Theory, Research & Practice.* San Francisco, California: Barrett-Koehler Publishers, 1993.

Cross, Elsie Y., Judith H. Katz, Frederick A. Miller, and Edith W. Seashore. *The Promise of Diversity: Over 40 Voices Discuss Strategies for Eliminating Discrimination in Organizations.* New York: Irwin Professional Publishing, 1994.

DesRoches, Brian, Ph.D. *Your Boss Is Not Your Mother: Breaking Free From Emotional Politics to Achieve Independence and Success at Work.* New York: Avon Books, 1995.

Diugan, Peter. "The Dangers of Multiculturalism: The American Experience." *Vital Speeches of the Day.* June 1, 1995.

Essed, Philomena. *Everyday Racism: Reports From Women of Two Cultures.* Clairmont, California: Hunter House, 1990.

Faludi, Susan. *Backlash: The Undeclared War Against American Women.* New York: Anchor Books, Doubleday, 1991.

Farrell, Warren. *Why Men Are the Way They Are.* New York: McGraw Hill, 1986

Federal Glass Ceiling Commission. "Good for Business: Making Full Use of the Nation's Human Capital. *The Environmental Scan.* Washington, D.C., 1995.

Fernandez, John P. *Managing a Diverse Work Force: Regaining the Competitive Edge.* Lexington, Massachusetts: D.C. Heath & Company, 1991.

Foster, Cecil. *A Place Called Heaven: The Meaning of Being Black in Canada.* Vancouver, Canada: Harper Collins, 1996.

Gardenswartz, Lee, and Anita Rowe. *Managing Diversity: A Complete Desk Reference and Planning Guide.* San Diego, California: Pfeiffer & Company, 1993.

Gates, Henry Louis, Jr. *Loose Cannons: Notes on the Culture Wars.* New York: Oxford University Press, 1992.

Gibson, Rowan. *Rethinking the Future: Rethinking Business, Principles, Competition, Control and Complexity, Leadership, Markets, and the World.* Sonoma, California: Nicholas Brealey Publishing, 1997.

Glass, Neil M. *Management Master Class: A Practical Guide to New Realities of Business.* London: Nicholas Brealey Publishing, 1996.

Goleman, Daniel. *Emotional Intelligence: Why It Can Matter More than IQ.* New York: Bantam Books, 1995.

Goreman, Tom. *Multipreneuring.* New York: Fireside, Simon & Schuster, 1996.

Guillory, William A. *The Business of Diversity: The Case for Action.* Innovations International Inc. 1994.

Hacker, Andrew. *Two Nations: Black, White, Separate, Hostile, Unequal.* New York: Ballantine Books, 1992.

Handy, Charles. *The Age Of Paradox.* Harvard Business School Press, 1994.

Handy, Charles. *Beyond Certainty.* Harvard Business School Press, 1996.

Hately, B. J., and Warren H. Schmidt. *A Peacock in the Land of Penguins.* San Francisco, California: Barrett-Koehler, 1995.

Hearny, Frances. *The Colour of Democracy: Racism in Canadian Society.* Vancouver, Canada: Harcourt Brace & Company, 1995.

Human Resource Management News. "Why Diversity Programs Miss the Mark." Chicago: Remy Publishing Company, 1993.

James, Jennifer. *Thinking in the Future Tense: Leadership Skills for a New Age.* New York: Simon Schuster, 1996.

Jamieson, David, and Julie O'Mara. *Managing Workforce 2000: Gaining the Diversity Advantage.* San Francisco: Jossey-Bass Publishers, 1991.

Jandt, Fred E. *Conflict Resolution Through Communication.* New York: Harper & Row, Publishers, 1973.

Jeffers, Susan, Ph.D. *Feel the Fear And Do It Anyway.* New York: Faucett Columbine, 1987.

Johnson, Sandra J. *Connect Diversity Efforts in the Workplace with Business Missions, Goals, and Objectives.* Performance Quality Management, 1994.

Kashmeri, Zuhair. *Web of Hate: Inside Canada's Far Right Network.* Vancouver, Canada: Harper Collins, 1996.

Knowdell, Richard L., Elizabeth Branstead, and Milan Moravec. *From Downsizing to Recovery: Strategic Transition Options for Organizations and Individuals.* Palo Alto, California: CPP Books, 1994.

Larsen, Earnie, and Jeanette Goldstein. *Who's Driving Your Bus? Codependent Business Behaviors of Workaholics, Perfectionists, Martyrs, Tap Dancers, Caretakers, and People-Pleasers.* San Diego: Pfeiffer & Company, 1993.

Lipman-Blumen, Jean. *Connective Edge: Leading in an Interdependent World.* San Francisco: Jossey-Bass Publishers, 1996.

Loden, Marilyn. *Implementing Diversity.* Chicago: Irwin Professional Publishing, 1996.

Loden, Marilyn, and Judy B. Rosener. *Workforce America! Managing Employee Diversity as a Vital Resource.* Homewood, Illinois: Business One Irwin, 1991.

Luttwak, Edward N. *The Endangered American Dream: How to Stop the United States from Becoming a Third-World Country and How to Win the Global-Economic Struggle for Industrial Supremacy.* New York: A Touchstone Book, published by Simon & Schuster, 1994.

Lynch, Frederick R. *The Diversity Machine: The Drive to Change the "White Male Workplace."* New York: The Free Press, A Division of Simon & Schuster, Inc., 1997.

Lynch, Frederick R. *Invisible Victim: White Males and The Crisis of Affirmative Action.* New York: Praeger, 1991.

Mauerer, Rick. *Feedback Toolkit: 16 Tools for Better Communication in the Workplace.* Portland, Oregon: Productivity Press, 1994.

McKay, Matthew, Ph.D., Martha Davis, Ph.D., and Patrick Fanning. *Messages: The Communication Skills Book.* Oakland, California: New Harbinger Press, Inc., 1995.

Milwid, Beth, Ph.D. *Working With Men: Professional Women Talk About Power, Sexuality, and Ethics.* Hillsboro, Oregon: Beyond Words Publishing, Inc., 1990.

Mobley, Michael, and Tamara Payne. "Backlash, The Challenge to Diversity Training." *Training and Development.* December, 1992.

Morrison, Ann M. *The New Leaders: Guidelines on Leadership Diversity in America.* San Francisco: The Jossey-Bass Management Series, 1992.

Morrison, Ann M., Randall P. White, Ellen Van Velsor, and the Center for Creative Leadership. *Breaking the Glass Ceiling: Can Women Reach the Top of America's Largest Corporations?* New York: Addison-Wesley Publishing, 1982.

Morrison, Toni. *Race-ing Justice, En-gendering Power: Essays on Anita Hill, Clarence Thomas, and the Construction of Social Reality.* New York: Pantheon Books, 1992.

Moynihan, Michael. *The Coming American Renaissance.* New York: Simon & Schuster, 1996.

National Association for Female Executives. *50/50 by 2000: The Woman's Guide to Political Power.* Berkeley, California: The EarthWorks Press, 1993.

Nichols, Michael P. *The Lost Art of Listening.* New York: The Guilford Press, 1995.

Office of the Inspector General. *The Tailhook Report: The Shocking Details Behind the Scandal That Has Rocked the Nation.* New York: St. Martin's Press, 1993.

Peters, Tom. *Liberation Management: Necessary Disorganization for the Nanosecond Nineties.* New York: Alfred A. Knopf, 1992.

Popcorn, Faith. *The Popcorn Report.* New York: Doubleday, 1996.

Popcorn, Faith, and Lys Marigold. *Clicking: 16 Trends to the Future to Fit Your Life, Your Work, and Your Business.* New York: Harper Collins, 1996.

Reed-Perkins, Marcia. *Thriving in Transition: Effective Living in Times of Change.* New York: Touchstone, 1996.

Roipe, Katie. *The Morning After Sex, Fear, and Feminism.* Black Bay Books, Little Brown and Company, 1994.

Rowan, Carl T. *The Coming Race War in America.* New York: Little Brown and Company, 1996.

Ryan, Kathleen D., and Daniel K. Oestreich. *Driving Fear Out of the Workplace: How to Overcome the Invisible Barriers to Quality, Production and Innovation.* San Francisco: Jossey-Bass Publishers, 1991.

Scott, Gini Graham, Ph.D. *Resolving Conflict: With Others and Within Yourself.* Oakland, California: New Harbinger Press, Inc. 1990.

Smith, Johnson, Nancy and Sylva K. Leduc. *Women's Work, Choice, Chance, or Socialization: Insights from Psychologists and Other Researchers.* Calgary, Alberta, Canada: Detselig Enterprises, Ltd., 1992.

Solomon, Charlene Marmer. "Global Operations Demand that Human Resources Rethink Diversity." *Personnel Journal.* July 1994.

Sowell, Thomas. *Race and Culture, A World View.* New York: Basic Books, A Division of HarperCollins Publishers, 1994.

Steele, Shelby. *The Content of Our Character: A New Vision of Race in America.* New York: St. Martin's Press, 1990.

Swiss, Deborah J. *Women Breaking Through: Overcoming the Final 10 Obstacles at Work.* Princeton, New Jersey: Peterson's/Pacesetter Books, 1996.

Tannen, Deborah, Ph.D. *Gender and Discourse.* New York: Oxford University Press, 1994.

Tannen, Deborah, Ph.D. *Talking from 9 to 5.* New York: William Morrow and Company, Inc., 1994.

Theobald, Robert. *The Rapids of Change: Social Entrepreneurship in Turbulent Times.* Indianapolis: Indiana: Knowledge Systems, Inc., 1987.

Thiederman, Sondra, Ph.D. *Bridging Cultural Barriers for Corporate Success: How to Manage the Multicultural Workforce.* New York: Lexington Books, 1991.

Thomas, Roosevelt R. *Beyond Race and Gender: Unleashing the Power of Your Total Work Force by Managing Diversity.* New York: American Management Association, 1991.

Thomas, Victor C. "The Downside of Diversity." *Training and Development.* 1994.

Tobias, Cynthia Ulrich. *The Way We Work: A Practical Approach for Dealing with People on the Job.* Colorado Springs, Colorado: Focus on the Family, 1995.

U.S. Conference Board. *Diversity Training: A Research Report.* Report #1083-94-RR, Washington, D.C., 1994.

U.S. Department of Labor Statistics. *Employment and Earnings.* Washington, D.C., September 1995.

U.S. Merit Systems Protection Board. *Sexual Harassment in the Federal Workplace—Trends, Progress, Continuing Challenges.* A Report to the President and Congress of the United States, Washington, D.C., 1995.

Urofsky, Melvin I. *A Conflict of Rights: The Supreme Court and Affirmative Action.* New York: Charles Scribner's Sons, 1991.

Weiss, Alan, Ph.D. *Our Emperors Have No Clothes: Incredibly Stupid Things Corporate Executives Have Done While Reengineering, Restructuring, Downsizing, TQMing, Team-building, and Empowering in Order to Cover Their Ifs, Ands or "Buts."* Franklin Lakes, New Jersey: Career Press, Inc., 1995.

White, Jane. *A Few Good Women: Breaking the Barriers to Top Management.* Englewood Cliffs, New Jersey: Prentice Hall, 1992.

Whyte, David. *The Heart Aroused.* New York: A Currency Paperback, published by Doubleday, 1994.

Williams, Roger John. *You are Extraordinary.* New York: Random House, 1967.

Zigarelli, Michael A. *Can They Do That? A Guide to Your Rights on the Job.* New York: Lexington Books, 1994.

Index

About the Authors

HELLEN HEMPHILL is President of Transitions Strategies, a transition management organization located in Bellevue, Washington. She is a transition management specialist, a psychologist, an author, an artist, and an educator. She is the former Dean of Women at Central Washington University.

RAY HAINES is Chief Executive Officer of Transitions Strategies and President of Haines Management Consulting and Training, Inc., both located in Bellevue, Washington. He has over thirty years of experience in business, project management, consulting, training, and education.